PRENTICE HALL

Language Teaching Methodology

Classroom Techniques and Resources

General Editor: Christopher N. Candlin

Pictures in Action

Other titles in this series include:

Pictures in Action

GÜNTER GERNGROSS and HERBERT PUCHTA

ENGLISH LANGUAGE TEACHING

Prentice Hall International
New York London Toronto Sydney Tokyo Singapore

First published 1992 by
Prentice Hall International (UK) Ltd
66 Wood Lane End, Hemel Hempstead
Hertfordshire HP2 4RG
A division of
Simon & Schuster International Group

Typeset in 10½/12½pt Times
by MHL Typesetting Ltd, Coventry

Printed and bound in Great Britain by
Dotesios Ltd, Trowbridge, Wiltshire.

Library of Congress Cataloging-in-Publication Data

Gerngross, Günter.
   Pictures in action / Günter Gerngross and Herbert Puchta.
      p.   cm. -- (Language teaching methodology series.)
   Includes indexes.
   ISBN 0-13-675182-2 : $17.00
    1. Pictures in education — United States — Handbooks, manuals, etc.
2. Language and languages — Study and teaching — United States —
Handbooks, manuals, etc. 3. Teaching — Aids and devices —
Handbooks, manuals, etc. 4. Activity programs in education —
United States — Handbooks, manuals, etc.
   I. Puchta, Herbert. II. Title. III. Series.
LB1043.67.G47   1992
371.3'352 — dc20   91-38683
                                       CIP

British Library Cataloguing in Publication Data

Gerngross, Günter
   Pictures in action. — (Language teaching
   methodology series — classroom teaching and
   resources)
   I. Title II. Puchta, Herbert III. Series
   428.007

   ISBN 0-13-675182-2

---

1 2 3 4 5 96 95 94 93 92

Contents

Preface

Within the Language Teaching Methodology Series we have created a special set of books with the *In Action* title. These books are designed to offer teachers material that can be directly used in class. They are resources for action, hence the title. They offer language teachers material which can be adapted with various inputs for their own classroom work. The activities are presented in an accessible and teacher-friendly way, with a clear identification of teacher and learner roles and above all, they consist of tried and tested tasks. The authors of the books in the *In Action* collection all have considerable practical experience of teaching and of classroom research. It is this combination of principle and practice available in an easily accessible form for the teacher which characterises the design of the books. We hope that they will not only help teachers to plan and carry out exciting lessons but also to develop themselves as reflective teachers by suggesting action research that can be done with their own learners.

In many ways, language learning is a process of understanding metaphors, looking at the way other worlds and other systems go about the familiar process of communicating ideas, values, opinions, preferences and beliefs. Language teaching, in turn, acts to provide keys to the unlocking of these complex metaphors, suggesting clues and ways of proceeding towards greater understanding. Such detective work has, of course, primarily to rest on our understanding of the verbal code, the words and structures which encode and realise the meanings that communication makes. None of us, however, relies on the form of words alone, whether oral or written. We draw upon all our iconic competence to picture the available and possible meanings of what people say and write. We make use of our visual sense to colour in the context against which words derive a part of their value. Pictures, then, are crucial to understanding, whether they are actual representations or images in the mind. Even Comenius knew that a very long time ago, when he wrote his *Pictures of the World*.

In this new book in the *In Action* collection, *Pictures in Action*, Günter Gerngross and Herbert Puchta draw on their immense practical classroom experience to offer readers a window into this world of images in language learning. Like other books in the collection, readers are provided with an easily accessible and catalogued set of practical classroom tasks, identified in relation to type of classroom activity, language-learning purpose and skill as well as level and competence of the learning group. It will be as easy to make use of individual activities as it will to chain them into a more extended curriculum. Moreover, the pictures themselves are equally varied: photographs, drawings, cartoons, classroom visual aids and commercial artwork are all brought into the collection of activities as models for teachers to extend and develop. There is especial value in the way that the authors tie various activities with pictures to particular communicative skills, both in speech and writing.

As General Editor, I hope that the books in this new *In Action* collection will continue the success of the Language Teaching Methodology Series more generally in developing the skills and knowledge of the reflective language teacher in the classroom.

Professor Christopher N. Candlin
General Editor

Acknowledgements

We should like to thank Erich Ballinger for allowing us to use his drawings (Activities 11, 22, 25, 26, 47, 51, 59, 62) and Peter Gerngross for many other drawings. Thanks to Judith Gaisch for her photos from East Asia.

INTRODUCTION

Introduction

The purpose of this book

Using pictures in the foreign-language class has a very long tradition. For many years, the main focus of the exploitation of visual stimuli has been on practising certain structures. Therefore generations of students have been presented with all sorts of pictures with the task of *describing what was going on* in a picture or *answering fake questions about* it. Clearly, questions like

> *What can you see in the picture?*
> *Is the tree bigger than the house?*
> *Is the girl holding a bag?*

force students to talk about the obvious. Asked in real life, these questions would certainly cause either laughter or confusion.

For whatever reason, there are still language classes in many parts of the world using pictures in this non-communicative way.

In real life, as opposed to the foreign-language class, we make communicative use of pictures in manifold ways. We show each other photographs of our latest holidays, we are surrounded by all sorts of visual stimuli in newspapers, in magazines and on TV, we consciously and subconsciously take in advertisements all the time. We go to museums and galleries.

The aim of this book is to show teachers how they can use pictures in order to make communication in the foreign-language class more lively, natural and stimulating. Moreover, we want to offer ideas on how to select pictures and use them in order to train specific areas of language. The activities focus on interaction in the classroom and combine learning language with practising social skills. Finally, experience has shown that the more senses are involved in the learning process, the better human memory works. With most learners, the visual sense is very important; as the saying goes: a picture is worth more than a thousand words. Our aim is to offer ideas in order to elicit 'a thousand words' from the learners stimulated by one or more pictures.

How to use this book

When you go to a restaurant you most likely have a good look at the menu before you order something to eat. If you belong to this category of consumer the indexes in *Pictures in Action* are what you want.

The indexes

1. Index of activities by picture type: a sequential listing of all the activities.

2. Index of skills: this will help you to select the activity for the skill or language area you wish to practise with your students.

3. Index of proficiency level: this will help you to select activities most suitable for the language level of your students.

Picture types

The activities in *Pictures in Action* are mainly based on authentic pictures and drawings, although classroom visual stimuli (blackboard drawings, flashcards, etc.) are taken into account occasionally. Categories — certainly not free of overlapping — include the following:

1. *Photographs from magazines or newspapers*: this very general category includes several different subcategories (portraits, action photographs, landscapes, objects, animals, etc.) Many of the activities in this book can be based on pictures taken from newspapers and magazines.

2. *Personal photographs*: pictures taken by the teacher, the students or someone else, and selected by the teacher or the students to be used in a particular activity.

3. *Drawings*: Another very broad category, including visual material like artwork, stickers, maps and the like.

4. *Cartoons*: generally used for humorous drawings, but could include picture stories, photo-romances, etc.

5. *Classroom visual aids*: all kinds of visual stimuli created for use in the classroom only.

6. *Commercial artwork*: any material which has been produced in order to attract potential customers, including visuals such as book covers and advertisements.

Activity types

The following categorisation gives an overview of teaching objectives that can be achieved by using the activities in *Pictures in Action*. Clearly, most activities serve more than one purpose.

1. *Sharing information*: this category of activities is based on the principle of the information gap, which means that students communicate with each other by mutually asking for and giving information.

2. *Sharing opinions*: activities which (based on an opinion gap between the speaker

and the listener) can be used in order to get students to exchange their views about a given topic.

3. *Developing short-turn talk*: activities focusing on helping students to ask questions, create and practise dialogues, take part in discussions, etc.

4. *Developing long-turn talk*: activities in which students narrate personal experiences or tell stories.

5. *Functional writing*: activities that involve the students in note-taking or note-making.

6. *Creative writing*: activities developing the students' written production, for example, by writing stories, inner monologues, poems, book blurbs, etc.

7. *Vocabulary*: activities focusing on the introduction of new vocabulary or the revision of language already presented.

8. *Listening skills*: activities focusing on what is said by the teacher or by classmates.

9. *Warm-ups*: activities that can best be done at the beginning of a lesson and help to establish a relaxed, inspired atmosphere.

10. *Grammar*: activities that focus on the presentation or review of certain grammatical structures.

11. *Developing social skills*: a very broad category that includes several of the above categories as subcategories, focusing on involving the students in social concerns, such as giving and receiving personal feedback, emphatic listening, etc.

Other criteria

Time

All the activities in *Pictures in Action* have been tried out in various classes. Trial classes range from highly motivated adults to adolescent learners or children, some of them showing a sad lack of motivation and interest. Since learners within the framework of compulsory education cause far more headaches for the teachers, we made sure that a large proportion of activities were tried out in 'difficult classes'. This has to be taken into account when selecting an activity according to the time given. Your class may work faster than the average trial class, they may work more slowly or may simply show greater or less interest in an activity, so that it may involve them for a longer or shorter period of time than indicated.

Function, grammar, vocabulary

These categories are only listed with activities which are aimed at practising specific language functions, grammatical structures or semantic areas. They help to select activities according to these criteria.

Preparation

Under this heading you will find suggestions on how to prepare to use an activity successfully in class. Here we have also included very practical things like glue and scissors that you might need to take along to your class.

In class

Although all the activities have been tried out and they have worked as presented here, we would like the reader to regard them as suggestions. The best use you can make of suggestions is to read them and be ready to change them, having in mind your class, their specific needs and your real-world constraints (size of class, availability of photocopier, OHP, etc.)

Alternative

Under this heading you will find alternative suggestions for individual steps of an activity.

Variation

This heading gives the reader alternative suggestions for the whole activity.

Action research element

A collection of experiences and authentic data from the trials of the activities. These include concrete hints, such as what the teacher in a certain trial class did at certain stages of the lesson in order to reach his/her goals, for example, to keep learners from falling back into their mother tongue. The reader will also find excerpts from lesson transcripts, photos of classroom situations and copies of texts produced by learners.

Selecting and storing pictures

With some of the activities in this book we offer photographs, pictures or drawings to be photocopied and used in class. This may be the quickest and easiest way to try out an activity. By offering visual stimuli we do not, of course, intend to keep the teachers from selecting visuals themselves.

Maybe you have seen an excellent picture that you thought you might like to use in your class but forgot to cut it out, or have perhaps looked in vain for good material, which in the end you could not find. In order to avoid this, we suggest that you start to select and collect pictures systematically. Magazines, newspapers (and especially their Sunday supplements), private photo collections, picture postcards, etc. are ideal stimuli for exciting lessons.

All you need is a pair of scissors, a simple filing system (cheap expanding files or wallets are an ideal means), glue and cardboard to stick the photographs on and make them re-usable. One more thing might be helpful: read through the activities in this book beforehand so that your eyes know what sort of visuals to look out for.

ACTIVITIES

1 Picture VIP

Types of picture:	Photos of very well known people or comic figures
Skill areas:	Speaking, listening
Grammar:	Questions
Functions:	Asking for information
Level:	Lower intermediate and above
Time:	10 minutes
Purpose:	This activity can be used as a warm-up

Preparation

Cut out photos of well-known people (drawings of comic figures) from newspapers or magazines (comic books), one for each learner. Prepare sellotape or a safety pin for each learner.

In class

1. Ask your class to sit in a circle. Hand out the photographs. Ask each learner to fix the photo on the back of his/her right-hand neighbour without the other person seeing the photograph.

2. Tell your class that everybody has the identity of the VIP whose photo they are carrying on their backs. Ask your learners to walk round and ask questions about their identity. Tell them that they are not allowed to ask one partner more than three questions. After asking three questions they have to change partners. Give some examples of questions. For example:

    Am I still living?
    Do I live in . . . ?
    Can people see me frequently on TV?
    Am I a real (fictional) person?
    etc.

Variation

This game can also be played with pictures of animals (*Do I live in Africa? Can I swim?* etc.) or objects.

> NOTE: *This is a variation of a game that has been around in the EFL world for quite a long time. It was impossible for us to trace the original source.*

2 Games with objects

Types of picture:	Objects
Skill areas:	Speaking, listening
Vocabulary:	Names of various objects
Grammar:	*Can you ...? Is it made of ...? Do you need ...? Comparison*
Functions:	Asking questions, giving reasons, narrating
Level:	Elementary and above
Time:	Two lessons of 20−30 minutes
Purpose:	To practise guessing, enhance creativity

Preparation

Cut out pictures of various objects from catalogues, magazines, newspapers, etc. and glue about twenty on to a poster. If your class is very large you will need several posters, one for a group of about twelve.

In class

First lesson

1. Present the names of the objects and practise them if necessary.

2. Ask a student to think of one object. Start guessing it. Do the same with several objects. Then ask them to work in pairs. Student A thinks of an object and B guesses it. Then they change roles. If there is a likelihood of your students' cheating, ask them to write down the words their partners have to guess.

Second lesson

3. Get the students to work in groups of four. They write down the three things

they would like to get as a birthday present. They start talking about the three things and give reasons for their choices.

4.   Group competition: students again work together in groups of four. Their task is now to tell a story in which as many objects as possible occur. The winners are the group that can convincingly pack most objects into the story. They are not, however, allowed to include lists in the story, for example, somebody going shopping and bringing back a lot of objects in a bag, or someone packing a suitcase, a person walking by a shop window looking at different objects, etc. Give them an example of a story in which several objects occur. Point out that in cases of uncertainty, you will decide whether to accept a story or not.

Action research element

At elementary level you might decide to do steps 1−3 only. Concerning step 2, we found it very useful in class to offer elementary students some help with the language of guessing. The content of the box below was either written on the board or presented on the OHP. When A and B in each pair had guessed several objects, the OHP was switched off or the teacher wiped the board clean.

Do you use it	at school? at home? outside? inside? every year? ...		Is it	cheap? expensive? red? blue? ...
Is it made of	leather? glass? wood? paper? plastic? metal? ...	Do you need it		every day? for sport? for your hobby? ...
Is it	smaller bigger longer shorter more expensive	than a ... ?		Can you wear it? Can you write with it? Can I see it in the classroom? Is it as big as a ... ?

3   Introducing new vocabulary to beginners

Types of picture:	Simple drawings on the board
Skill areas:	Listening, speaking
Level:	Elementary
Time:	10 minutes
Purpose:	To introduce vocabulary; to anchor new words in the students' minds in a multi-sensory way (visually, auditorily and kinesthetically)

Preparation

Prepare flashcards with the new words written on them. You may also want to prepare drawings of the words on cards or quickly sketch simple drawings on the board. Bring blu-tack or sellotape.

In class

1. Show the drawings to the learners one after the other, or quickly draw on the board. Elicit from the learners any words that they can come up with, even if the words they give you are not the ones you are aiming at. For example, when the picture you have drawn is 'sausage', and a learner says 'In a hot dog', accept this and praise the learner for it. ('Right, it's in a hot dog. Very good.' etc.) Do not give the words at this stage yet.

2. Quickly flash the cards with the words written on them to your learners. You can even try holding them upside down or sideways while you are flashing the words to your class. Do not correct pronunciation, but indicate that it is not correct and flash the card again and again until someone in the class gets the word right. When a learner has 'guessed' the correct pronunciation, give the card to this learner and ask him or her to fix it beneath the drawing s/he thinks it belongs to. If the student gets it wrong, ask someone else to match word and drawing. Continue until all the words are fixed underneath the drawings they belong to.

3. Point at the words one after the other again and pronounce them clearly.

4. Ask your learners to close their eyes and to listen to you pronouncing all the words on the board again.

5. Ask your learners to repeat each word after you with their eyes closed. Ask them to imitate you as closely as possible. Vary your voice (whisper, shout, talk in a high pitch, etc.) and get your learners to talk in the same way.

6. Tell your learners to open their eyes. Mouth the words, ask your learners to guess the word you have said by reading your lips.

7. Ask the learners to close their eyes, and then remove one word card from the board. Ask 'What's missing?' Continue with the rest of the words.

8. Remove all the word cards from the board. Ask the learners to remember the words. Whenever they remember a word correctly, ask a learner to fix the word card for this word back on the board again.

9. Write numbers against each word card plus drawing. Tell your students that they have one minute to concentrate on the word cards and the drawings. Ask them to remember the numbers together with the respective words. Tell them that you are going to ask them to close their eyes in a minute and then call out a number. They should then be able to give you the matching word.

10. Ask them to close their eyes. Say a number and wait for the words.

    Variation: Say the word, your learners give you the number.

4 Nonsense pictures

Types of picture:	Nonsense drawings
Skill areas:	Speaking, listening, reading, writing
Vocabulary:	Objects, locations
Grammar:	Prepositions
Functions:	Describing pictures
Level:	Lower intermediate and above
Time:	60 minutes
Purpose:	Describing a picture orally and in writing

Preparation

You need at least two nonsense pictures for each member of your class.

In class

1. Ask a student to come to the board. 'Dictate' a nonsense picture, which the student draws on the board.

2. Now tell your students to work in pairs. Hand out one nonsense picture to each student A and another one to each student B. They must not show their pictures to their partners. Then A starts to dictate his/her picture to his/her partner B, who draws according to A's orders. When A has finished giving orders, they compare the pictures. Then it is B's turn to dictate his/her picture to A.

3. Hand out another nonsense picture each to A and B. Again they must not show their pictures to one another. Now the task for A and B is to describe in writing the pictures in detail. When they have finished, their descriptions are handed over to their partners, who try to draw the nonsense pictures following the written

instructions of their partners. When they have finished drawings, the students compare what they have drawn with the original pictures.

Sample drawings

 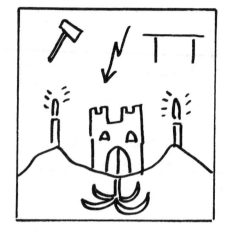

5 Happy moments

Types of picture:	Learners bring photos of themselves taken in a situation in which they were happy
Skill areas:	Speaking, listening
Vocabulary:	As related to content of picture
Grammar:	Past tense
Functions:	Narrating, asking for information
Level:	Lower intermediate and above
Time:	30–40 minutes
Purpose:	Students remember a situation in which they felt happy, and share this experience in class

Preparation

Ask your learners to bring to class a photo of themselves in a situation in which they felt happy, no matter how old they were when the photo was taken and no matter what the situation was. Tell them not to show their photographs to any other member of the class or talk about the situation in which the photograph was taken.

In class

1. Ask your learners to sit with their chairs in a circle. Ask them to put their photographs on the floor. Pick up one photograph, ask whose it is and hand it round the circle. Get your students to imagine little background stories to the photograph. If they find this difficult at first, give an example; for instance, Maria, this photograph shows you at the beach, probably with some friends. I think when this picture was taken, you were about seventeen years old. You seem to be excited, because you were going to have a barbecue and a beach party.

2. After several interpretations of the picture have been heard, ask the student whose picture it is to explain what the situation was really like. Then everybody has a chance to ask this student some more questions about the picture.

3. Proceed like this with all the photos on the floor. If there are more than ten students in the group, split them up after two or three examples have been given and have them work in two or more smaller groups.

4. As a follow-up activity you could ask each learner to bring another photograph with similar emotional impact. Collect the photos and hand them out again so that everybody gets somebody else's photograph. Then tell your students to write a short narrative text about the situation. Hand a photo round and ask the student who wrote a narrative text about it to read it out. Then ask the owner of the photograph to tell his or her story.

Variation to follow-up activity (step 4)

Ask the learners to stick the photos and the text they have produced on the wall, next to each other. Then the owners of the photographs write their own short narratives about their photos and stick them next to the other text and the photo. Have your learners walk round and read as many texts as possible.

Action research element

In all the classes where we have tried out this activity, learners have commented on it very positively. It seems that memories of happy moments help to recall the feelings we had in these situations. For these reasons, the activity described above lends itself ideally to being used as a confidence builder in classes which have only been together for a short period of time.

6 Jumbled pictures

Types of picture:	Picture stories, cartoons
Skill areas:	Speaking, listening
Functions:	Describing pictures
Level:	Lower intermediate and above
Time:	40 minutes
Purpose:	To stimulate talking and intensive listening

Preparation

One copy of a cut-up picture story for each group of students. The size of the groups depends on the number of pictures in the story; for example, if there are six pictures in a story, you will need four copies for twenty-three students. In three groups each student gets one picture, in the fourth group one student gets two.

In class

1. Write some key words of the story on the board. Ask your students to develop a story from the words. Have them tell the stories to the class.

2. Hand out the pictures. Make sure that the learners are aware of the fact that they must not show their picture(s) to the others. Each student describes his/her picture and then they decide in what order to arrange them. When they have negotiated the order they put the pictures in a line, face down. The advantage of this step is that more language is elicited: 'What was the picture you've just put down like, Sergio? — It's the one . . .'

3. The groups usually do not finish at the same time. When the first group has finished, the teacher goes from group to group and they quietly tell the story. This gives the group a chance to rehearse retelling. When all the groups have finished, the first group tells their story, and only then are the pictures turned over. A discussion may follow if a group has developed a different order.

Sample story

When a hat-maker has made enough hats to sell, he puts them on a barrow and starts out for the market in town. On his way there, he stops to rest under a tree, since it is very hot. In the tree there are several monkeys, who climb down to get the hats as soon as the hat-maker has fallen asleep. When the hat-maker wakes up he sees the empty barrow, but when he looks around he knows who the thieves are. When he angrily shakes his fist at the monkeys, they do the same. That gives the hat-maker an idea. He throws his hat on the ground, and luckily the monkeys copy him again. He only has to collect his hats and then he can continue his way to the market.

Sample pictures

Action research element

The key words for the sample story that was used in class were: *hat-maker, tree, monkeys, town, barrow, trick.*

With lower intermediate groups, we find it very helpful to write useful language for negotiation on the board to show it on the OHP.

> *It's your turn.*
> *This can't be the next picture because ...*
> *In my picture the ... has got (can't, isn't ...) ...*
> etc.

NOTE: *We heard the story from Edie Garvie at a conference in Vienna in 1991.*

7 Judge a book by its cover

Types of picture: Book cover

Skill areas: Writing a blurb, reading comprehension, speaking

Functions: Reporting about one's reading habits; language of speculation

Level: Intermediate and above

Time: 40–50 minutes

Purpose: Involving the students in a discussion about what they read; blurb writing

Preparation

Select a book cover that is likely to arouse your students' interest. It should not be a book that is familiar to your class.

In class

1. Involve your students in a discussion about their reading habits. A few guiding questions might facilitate this discussion, for example:

   Do you like reading (If not, why not?)
   How many books do you read a year?
   What do you read?
   Where do you get your books from?
   Do you often go to libraries/bookshops?
   What are your favourite types of book?
   What is your favourite book?
   What is your favourite time for reading?
   What is your favourite place of reading?

2. Explain to your class what the blurb of a book is. Show them a book or two and slowly read out their blurbs. Then show them the cover of another book you have

selected without giving them a chance to read the blurb. Ask them to guess from the title and the cover of the book what they think this book is all about (type of book, setting, characters, plot, target audience, etc.). They should then write a blurb for this book.

3. Ask your learners to read out the blurbs they have written and finally read out the authentic blurb.

4. As a follow-up activity in future lessons, your learners might enjoy writing reviews about books they have recently read or reporting orally about their favourite books.

Sample book cover

Action research element

This is the blurb written by an intermediate student for the sample book cover above. Compare the student's blurb with the original blurb.

Student's blurb

Sam Brown is a fourteen-year-old boy, who goes to school in New York. He doesn't like school because he thinks that most of his teachers are unfair to him. There is one big problem Sam has. He can't read very well. That's why he has bad marks in most subjects. One day when he's roaming the streets he spots a book lying in the gutter. He picks it up. Its title is, 'The day they came to arrest the book'. Sam doesn't understand what that means, but he is interested, sits down on a park bench and begins to read the book. It is very hard, but later he asks a friend to help him and gradually he begins to understand what the book is all about. And the story in the book seems very familiar to him, it is like his own story.

But is the story in the book really Sam's story? Or does Sam just imagine it is. The answer to that question can be found in the book.

Original blurb

Censored! Who ever heard of a literary classic being banned from school? Well, that's just what happens at the George Mason High School, when a small group of parents and students brand Huckleberry Finn *as racist, sexist and immoral, and persuade the principal to remove it from the library shelves.*

But that's just the beginning of the story: soon the book's future becomes a burning issue, as parents, students and teachers rush to take sides. Readers too will find plenty to agree and disagree with in this provocative and witty portrait of a community in conflict.

> *NOTE: The idea for this activity came from Christian Holzmann.*

8 My favourite picture

Types of picture:	Drawings done in class or photos brought to the class by students
Skill areas:	Speaking, listening
Functions:	Giving reasons, describing, guessing
Level:	Lower intermediate and above
Time:	40 minutes
Purpose:	Talking about things that are meaningful to oneself

Preparation

Sheets of paper for drawing or photos brought to the class by the students themselves.

In class

1. The teacher draws three items on the blackboard, for example a book, contact lenses, a landscape, etc. and tells the learners that they mean a lot to him/her. The students now start guessing what the items represent and what they mean to the teacher. With the examples given above it is obvious that it will take them some time to figure out that two small circles represent contact lenses, but their importance for the teacher is rather obvious. On the other hand, it is easy to recognise the landscape, but it could be far more difficult to guess its meaning for the teacher.

   Example: The teacher draws a book on the board.

   STUDENT 1: *Is it a book you got from a very good friend?*
   TEACHER: *No, it isn't.*
   STUDENT 2: *Is it the first book you read?*
   TEACHER: *No, it isn't. I've only had it for two years.*
   STUDENT 3: *Is it the book you like best?*
   TEACHER: *No, I like it a lot, but it isn't the book I like best.*
   STUDENT 4: *Was it expensive?*

TEACHER: *Yes. And it has got something to do with the author.*
STUDENT: *Did the author write something in it?*
TEACHER: *Yes, that's it. It's a copy with the author's autograph.*

2.   The students work in small groups of three to five. Learners who know each other very well should not work together. They draw three items on their sheets.

3.   The students show their drawings in turn to the other participants in their groups, who start guessing what the items are. When they have found that out, they go on guessing what the items mean to the person presenting them. The learner presenting his/her drawings comments on the guesses.

Example:

A: *Yes, it's a board game. It's called Abalone.*
B: *Is it important for you because you got it from a close friend?*
A: *No, that's not the reason.*
C: *Do you play it very often?*
A: *Yes, that's right.*
C: *Is it important for you because you like playing it with close friends.*
A: *Close friends is not right.*
C: *Your brothers or sisters?*
A: *Yes, that's it. I often play it with my sister and we keep track of who is in the lead.*

Alternative: The students bring their favourite photos. There is usually no guesswork about what the photo shows. The focus of interest is on what the item presented means to the respective learner.

Variation

The teacher draws three items on the board and tells the learners that they have got something to do with what he/she would like to do, would like to have, would like to experience, etc. The learners do the guess work and then work in groups as described above.

9   What's s/he wearing?

Types of picture:	Full-page photos from fashion magazine showing full-length pictures of men or women
Skill areas:	Speaking, listening
Vocabulary:	Clothes, colours, adjectives describing clothes
Grammar:	Present progressive
Functions:	To guess what clothes a person is wearing
Level:	Elementary
Time:	20 minutes
Purpose:	To practise present progressive and revise vocabulary: clothes

Preparation

Cut out some full-page photos as described above. Glue them on cardboard.

In class

1. If necessary, introduce vocabulary for clothes. Use real clothes, show them on your learners or draw on the board to make the meaning of the words clear. In the same way, explain colours and words like striped, check, etc.

2. Ask one of the learners to come out to the front. Stand back to back with this learner and ask 'What am I wearing?' The student has to guess your clothes. Help him or her by prompting and asking further questions; for example:

TEACHER: *What am I wearing?*
STUDENT: *I think you are wearing a jacket.*
TEACHER: *Right. What colour is it?*
STUDENT: *Blue?*
TEACHER: *Mmh. And what else am I wearing?* etc.

When the teacher feels that enough guesses have been made, the learner and the teacher turn around to face each other. The learners then usually tend to comment on what sort of mistakes they have made.

3.   Ask all your learners to mill around in the classroom. At a given sign, they should stand back to back with a partner. They should not get any time to check what their partner is wearing. Ask them to guess their partners' clothes without looking. It may be necessary to tell them to close their eyes.

4.   Stand in front of the class. Hold one of the pictures you have prepared between your thumbs and index fingers with it's back to the class. Quickly flick it over so that the class can see the picture for a moment only. While you are doing this, ask 'What's s/he wearing?' Get your students to guess exactly what the person is wearing. If necessary, show them the picture for a moment a second or third time. Continue with the rest of the pictures or ask individual learners to take over from you.

10 While and after

Types of picture:	Pictures of people doing something
Skill areas:	Speaking, listening, writing
Grammar:	Past continuous, past perfect
Functions:	Contrasting events, talking about events before a particular time in the past
Level:	Lower intermediate and above
Time:	20 minutes
Purpose:	Grammar review

Preparation

Cut out pictures as specified above. Glue them on to pieces of cardboard.

In class

1. Hold a picture with the blank side towards the class and turn it over a couple of times very quickly so that your learners have to guess its content. If some of the words for the actions shown in the pictures are not known to the class, preteach the words using mime, gestures, etc. before flashing the pictures.

2. Stick a picture on the board (e.g. a couple having dinner) and write the following sentence below:

   While they were having dinner, something embarrassing happened. ...
   dreadful
   unexpected
   funny

Give your students an example for each situation.

TEACHER: *While they were having dinner in a restaurant, something*

> *embarrassing happened. The man started slurping down his*
> *soup so loudly that some other guests turned their heads.*

While . . . unexpected happened. Suddenly the lights went out. Some people started
to panic.
While . . . dreadful happened. The waiter stumbled and poured the hot soup into
the woman's lap.
While . . . funny happened. When the man tried to fork a mushroom on his plate,
it sailed across the room and a dog that was lying under one of the tables
snapped it up.

3. Then show them several pictures (e.g. a man buying something); stick them on
    the board and ask them to write about one situation. Give another example.

    While he was buying some cheese, something unexpected happened. The salesgirl
    smelled the cheese and fainted.

4. The students read out their texts.

5. At some later stage the same pictures can be used to practise the past perfect.
    Stick a picture on the board and write the following beneath it.

    When she had got on the bus, something (embarrassing/dreadful/etc.) happened.

6. Elicit some ideas from your students. Then stick several pictures on the board
    and ask them to write short texts.

    Example:
    When he had fed the cat, something dreadful happened. The cat seemed to grow;
    it growled, turned and jumped at him.

11 Excuse me, where's the cafeteria?

Types of picture:	Map
Skill areas:	Listening, speaking
Vocabulary:	Buildings and places in a town, university campus, etc.
Grammar:	Present simple
Functions:	Asking and telling the way
Level:	Elementary
Time:	10–15 minutes
Purpose:	Asking for and giving information

Preparation

Copy each of the two maps below for half the number of your students or select or draw a map (city centre, university campus, etc). Photocopy this map twice. Then tippex ten different items from each map (do not erase the buildings, but their designations). On the margin of each of the two maps, list the buildings whose designations you have removed under 'Ask for'.

In class

1. Organise your students into pairs. Tell them to imagine that one of them is a tourist, the other one a local (or a new and a senior student on a university campus). Give them two minutes to become familiar with the map they have been given. It is essential that students only look at their own and not their partners' maps.

2. Get the students to ask each other for the location of the items removed from their maps. The students note down in their maps where these items are located.

3. Check the students' work by acting as someone who is a tourist yourself. In turn,

ask each half of the class about the location of buildings and places that they did not originally have in their maps, but that they have learnt about from their partners.

Sample worksheets A and B

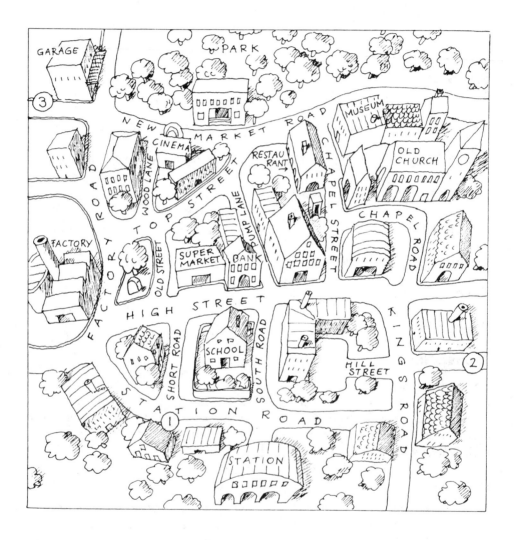

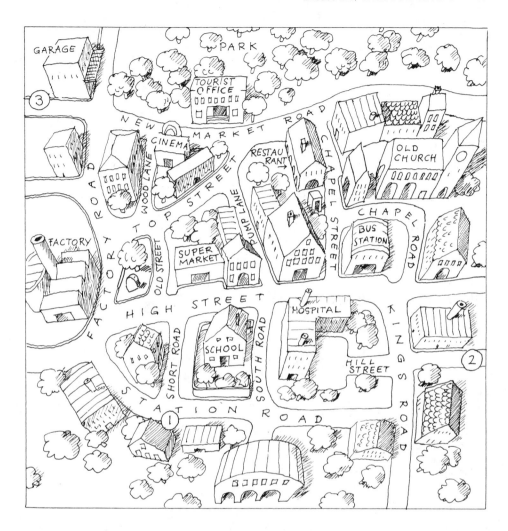

NOTE: *The idea for this activity is taken from Peter Watcyn-Jones,* Pair Work One *(Penguin Functional Englisy, 1984).*

12 Yummy

Types of picture:	A large number of photos, drawings of food and dishes
Skill areas:	Speaking, listening
Vocabulary:	Related to food
Grammar:	Questions
Functions:	Asking questions
Level:	Elementary
Time:	20 minutes
Purpose:	Talking about food, introduction and revision of vocabulary

Preparation

Pictures of food and dishes.

In class

1. Preteach vocabulary using all the photos. You could also play the guessing game: 'I'm thinking of something to eat beginning with "c"', etc.

2. Have your pupils sit in a semi-circle and put all the photos on the floor in front of them. Ask one student to think of an item and then guess it yourself.

   Example:
   Is it something you eat/drink? Is it sweet/savoury? Is it made of grain/milk? Is it a fruit/vegetable/meat? Do you eat it raw? Do you have to cook it? Is it soft/hard/green/red/etc.?

   Do this a couple of times so that your students pick up the relevant language to allow them to guess effectively. Then pick one item yourself and ask them to guess it.

3. Collect all the pictures and hand one to each student. Ask them to work in pairs. They are not allowed to show the pictures to their partners. Ask them to start the guessing game. When a pair has finished tell them to swap their pictures with another pair that has also finished.

4. Then ask the students to write down on a piece of paper their favourite fruit, their favourite meat and their favourite vegetables, b"t make sure that their partners cannot see what they have written. The activity is a competition. The aim is to find out about their partners' favourite meat/fruit/vegetables. The winner is the one who needs fewer guesses to find out their partners' favourite food. Demonstrate the activity by having one student ask you: 'Is your favourite fruit apples?' etc. When the student has found out your favourite fruit tell him/her to ask for your favourite meat and vegetable as well. Count the guesses s/he needs.

When they have done the activity in pairs, get them to report their partners' favourite food back to the class: 'John's favourite fruit is . . ., his favourite meat is . . . and his favourite vegetable is . . . .'

13   What a dream!

Types of picture:	An unreal, mysterious painting, picture or drawing. Reproductions of paintings by Carlo Carra, Salvador Dali, Giorgio de Chirico, René Magritte are very suitable
Skill areas:	Writing, reading aloud, listening
Grammar:	Past tense
Functions:	Narrating
Level:	Lower intermediate and above
Time:	40 minutes
Purpose:	Story telling

Preparation

Pictures as specified above.

In class

1. Hand out photocopies of the sample picture or one you have chosen and tell your students that the picture shows a dream someone had. Ask them to make some guesses concerning the dream. Then tell them a story of a dream:

    Riding a snake
    A dentist (Jerry) falls in love with a patient: young woman, Suzanne. Takes her out, buys fast car, tried to impress her. Suzanne tells him she likes him, doesn't love him. Dentist — Jerry — hurt, looks for another girlfriend. Suzanne works with snakes in zoo. One day snake bites her, Suzanne takes medicine, then faints. Has dream: huge twisting snake throws man into sea, man's face: Jerry. Suzanne worried, rings up Jerry, no answer, rings friend. Friend: Jerry in the south of France with girlfriend. Some days later friend rings again, Jerry dead, accident, car shot into sea.

2. Hand out another picture (stick it on the wall) and tell your students to write a

story in which a dream — represented by the picture — plays an important part.

3. Students read out their stories.

Variation

Have them write their texts as chain stories. They work in groups of seven or eight and use the same picture as a stimulus. Each student writes down a sentence — the beginning of the story — and then they all pass on their texts to their left-hand neighbours. They read what has been written down and continue the story by writing another sentence. The rule for each round is that not more than two sentences should be written by an individual student. When the stories come back to the ones who started them, they round them off and give them titles. All the stories are then read out.

Sample picture

14 Remember their actions

Types of picture: A drawing containing a number of stick people carrying out different sorts of actions

Skill areas: Speaking and listening

Vocabulary: Various actions

Grammar: Present continuous, *there is, there are*

Functions: Emphasising the present moment

Level: Elementary

Time: 30 minutes

Purpose: Grammar review

Preparation

Bring copies of the drawing described above.

In class

1. Hand out copies of the picture described above (see sample drawing) or use an OHP transparency. To check on vocabulary, ask your students to name all the verbs. Write words unknown to the students on the board.

2. Ask them to work in pairs.

   (a) Both students have the picture in front of them.
       STUDENT 1: *I'm thinking of a person in the picture.*
       STUDENT 2: *Is it a man?*
       STUDENT 1: *Yes, it is.*
       STUDENT 2: *Is he eating an apple?* etc.

   (b) Again both students have the picture in front of them.
       STUDENT 1: *I'm one of the people in the picture. Guess what I'm doing.*

STUDENT 2:   *Are you playing football?*
etc.

(c) One student puts his/her picture into the desk or a folder etc. If you use the OHP, one student (A) in a pair turns his/her chair so that he/she is sitting with his/her back to the OHP. A now tries to describe the picture from memory: a woman is writing a letter; two men are skiing; etc. After some time the pair change roles: A looks at the OHP (the copy of the picture) and B now tries to recall the actions without looking at the OHP or the worksheet.

Variation

(c) Students use the following structure:

There is a woman skiing, there are two men playing cards, etc.

At a later point you could use the same material to elicit structures expressing the past.

The students try to remember what the pictures showed using either *A man and a woman were riding their bikes*, etc. or *There were two men and two women dancing. There was ...*

Sample drawing

NOTE: *Andrew Wright's* 1000 Pictures for Teachers to Copy *(Collins, 1984) is an excellent source to teach you how to draw stick people.*

15 Do the stories match?

Types of picture:	Any
Skill areas:	Listening, writing
Functions:	Narrating
Level:	Intermediate and above
Time:	40–60 minutes, depending on the size of the class
Purpose:	Creative writing using a picture or a set of words as stimulus

Preparation

Cut out pictures that lend themselves to story telling from newspapers and magazines.

In class

1. Ask your students to call out ten words, and write them on the board. Tell them a story using all the words.

2. Show your students several pictures and ask them to choose one. Use that picture to tell a story around it.

3. Split your class into two groups (A and B).
    Group A: each of them should choose one picture from a pile you have prepared and write a story around it. In order to give the students a real choice, there should be far more pictures than learners. When the students have selected their pictures, quickly check which pictures have *not* been taken.
    Group B: Hand out cards to each member of group B. On each card there are about ten words. Each card is related to one picture in the pile group A chose their pictures from. Tell group B that they should write a story using the words on their cards. Make sure to remove the cards that go with the pictures that were *not* taken by group A.

Example: Picture: a very old man from an African tribe is handing something one cannot see to a much younger man who is looking carefully and maybe a bit suspiciously at the old man's hand. The background of the picture is blurred.

On the card that went with that picture there were the following words: *old chief, young chief, Africa, magic stone, little food, help, happy, far away*.

4. When the members of groups A and B have finished writing their stories, the pictures are stuck on the wall one by one for everybody to see. For each picture, ask the student who chose it to read out the story. Then ask if anybody in group B has got a story that might go with the picture. If there is one, get the student to read it out as well.

5. If there are any group B students left who have not been able to match their stories with a picture, ask them to read out their texts too, and make the others guess which picture might fit.

Alternative: When the students have finished writing their stories, ask them to stick the pictures on the wall and place the stories that go with them beneath them. Then ask the members of group B to walk around and stick their stories next to the picture they think goes with the words on their cards.

16 True or false?

Types of picture: Any, preferably with lots of details

Skill areas: Listening, speaking, reading

Grammar: Present progressive, prepositions

Functions: Language of description

Level: Elementary

Time: 30—40 minutes

Purpose: Listening comprehension, note taking

Preparation

Select a picture and photocopy it so that there is one copy for each pair of students.

In class

1.   Get your students to work in pairs. Hand out a copy of the picture to each pair. Tell your class to study the picture and remember as many details as possible. Allow two minutes for that, then ask them to put their pictures face down on their desks.

2.   Hand out a dictionary to each pair so that your students can look up any words related to the picture that they do not know in English.

     Alternative: The students ask for the English equivalents of the words they do not know and the teacher lists all the words asked for on the board or on poster paper.

3.   Read out once only a list of about twenty sentences related to the picture. Some of these sentences should be false in regard to the picture. The students are not allowed to take any notes.

     Examples of sentences that could be used for working with the sample picture opposite:

Altogether there are seven people to be seen.
Two people are holding a walking stick.
Apart from two people, they are all looking in the same direction.
There is a plastic container under the bench on the right.
There are more men than women.
The man without the glasses is wearing a hat.
The woman with the walking stick has got sunglasses.
The man who has got a wrist watch on his left hand is smiling.
There are two people who are not holding a bag in their hands.
Five people are wearing dark shoes.
One of the two women on the middle has got a bunch of flowers in her hands.
The man on the left has got a moustache.
The man who has got a jacket on is wearing a tie.
There are some bottles in the window behind the group of people on the left.
There is a cat next to the bench on the left.

4. Get your students to work in pairs and try to remember as many sentences as possible. Each pair should note these sentences down. Get them to decide whether they think each sentence is true or false.

5. Ask your students to write down on the right-hand side of the blackboard sentences

they think are true and on the left-hand side sentences they think are false. Do not interfere even if there are language errors in the students' sentences.

6. Without speaking, tick all the sentences that have been put in the right column and are linguistically correct.

7. Use mime and gesture to signal to the students that the sentences you have not ticked are not absolutely correct. Get them to work on these sentences. Do not tell them verbally what is wrong about each sentence but again help them with mime and gesture. Whenever they get a sentence right go to the board and tick it.

Variation

Read out twenty sentences that express your opinion about things going on in the picture. Again the students should not write these sentences down immediately (as in a dictation), but they should remember as many of the sentences as they can, and after you have finished reading them out, note them down. Then get them to agree or disagree with the opinion expressed in each sentence. This could be done in pairs or small groups.

Examples of opinions to be given with the sample picture:

The people in the photograph are all sceptically watching something.
The man and the woman on the left are a married couple.
The picture was not taken in an English-speaking country.
The group of people on the right have just had a quarrel.
etc.

Action research element

It is valuable for the teacher to include words in the sentences that are presumably new to the learners. Getting these words right in the end can increase motivation and give the students an immediate positive feedback on the efficiency of their reference skills.

17 Collages

Types of picture:	Pictures of locations, objects and people
Skill areas:	Speaking, listening, writing
Functions:	Narrating
Level:	Intermediate and above
Time:	50 minutes
Purpose:	Telling and writing stories, enhancing creativity

Preparation

On stiff paper (35 × 50 cm), glue five to eight pictures containing locations, people and objects in order to create a 'collage'. You will need one collage for each group of three.

In class

1. Put the collages up on the wall of your classroom. Ask your students to work in groups of three and to have a look at the collages. Tell them that their task is to tell (write) a story using all the pictures in their collage.

2. Ask the students to choose a collage and to take it back to their places. Get them to discuss their ideas and to prepare to tell their stories.
   Alternative: They write the stories down.

3. When they have finished, ask one group to start telling their story. Suggest taking turns when telling the story. If they have written a story, have one of the group read it out.

Variation

You might choose to use one or two collages only. Stick them on the wall and ask the teams to look closely at them. They should, of course, have the opportunity to have another look at the collage when putting together their story.

47

Action research element

With some adult classes we have found it far easier to have them write down their stories. When we asked them to tell stories, some of the groups said after about fifteen minutes that they had not been able to think of a good story. This never happened when they were made to write them down.

18   From symbols to poems

Types of picture:	Symbolic drawings or pictures of emotional impact
Skill areas:	Creative writing, reading out aloud, listening
Level:	Intermediate and above
Time:	60 minutes
Purpose:	Students create a word field based on a visual stimulus and create poems

Preparation

Select non-rhyming poems appropriate for the level of your class. Photocopy the poems if you wish to hand them out to your learners. Draw meaningful symbolic drawings on large sheets of poster paper. These symbols should be likely to activate the learners' creativity (see the examples below). Collect lots of magazines, Sunday newspapers, supplements, etc. Bring these, poster paper, glue sticks, felt tips and several pairs of scissors to class.

In class

1. Read out some poems or hand out photocopies of them. They should make it obvious to your students that the term 'poem' is not restricted to highly polished works of art but that poetry comes in a great variety of forms. Learners should get a feeling that they can write poetry too.

2. Stick the large sheets of poster paper with the symbols on the wall. Ask your learners to get together in pairs or groups of three to four each. Each group should work with one poster.

3. Get your students to write down their associations with their symbol on the poster paper. They could also draw, cut out pictures from the magazines and stick them on the poster paper. Thus your students are likely to get into a creative, playful mood. Play some meditative music while the students are working.

4. After about fifteen minutes ask students to sit down and write a poem based on the ideas in the poster they have created. Remind them that their poems need not rhyme.

5. Walk round the class and discreetly help your learners with language problems in their poems. Later, display all the poems on a poetry board together with the poems you read out in step 1. In a follow-up lesson get your students to talk about how they perceived this lesson and also about the poems they wrote.

Sample symbols

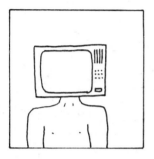

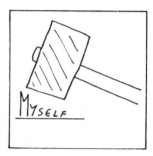

Action research element

The following poems have been used successfully in order to stimulate the learners' creativity:

Happiness is the colour of red flowers.
It smells like the flowers in a small garden.
Happiness sounds like the singing of a hippo in the water.
Happiness makes me dance rock and roll.

What's black?

The frozen leg
of the soldier,
the burnt tree,
the seabird in the oilslick,
the river of poison
and the mushroom cloud
in the sky.

I'd rather be the sea than a ship
I'd rather be a kite than a plane
I'd rather be a path than a road
I'd rather be a blackbird than a toad
Yes I would
If I could.

NOTE: *This activity is part of a project on writing poetry with secondary learners. It is taken from H. Puchta and M. Schratz,* Teaching Teenagers *(Pilgrims—Longman, 1992).*

---

19 Funny ads

Types of picture:	Objects, shops, restaurants, food, plants
Skill areas:	Speaking, listening, reading and writing
Functions:	Language of exaggeration
Level:	Intermediate and above
Time:	30 minutes
Purpose:	Creative writing

Preparation

Cut out pictures as specified above from magazines and have some poster paper ready. Bring some glue.

In class

1. Hand out copies of one or two examples of funny ads and ask your learners to read them.

2. Now offer your learners a great choice of pictures from which they should choose one as a stimulus for writing a funny ad. Ask them to work in teams of three, to stick the pictures on poster paper and to write the text beneath them. Make yourself available to help with the language.

3. The funny ads are then displayed in the classroom. The students mill around and read as many as possible.

Action research element

This activity worked very well as a competition. When all the posters had been displayed in the classroom, each team read each ad. The teams gave points (5 points for the ad they liked best, 4 points for the next best, etc.). The team with the most points got a prize.

Sample ad

The Hungry Hippo

NOTE: *The Hungry Hippo was taken from: G. Gerngross, H. Puchta and M. Schratz,* English for You and Me 4 *(Langenscheidt−Longman, 1988).*

20 The person behind the sticker

Types of picture:	Sticker or photo of sticker
Skill areas:	Reading, listening, speaking, writing
Grammar:	Questions
Functions:	Asking for opinions, persuading someone, language of argumentation
Level:	Intermediate and above
Time:	30−40 minutes
Purpose:	Development of discoursal competence, language of speculation and argumentation, empathy with other people

Preparation

Copy for each student one or all four of the stickers below or bring a provocative sticker to class.
Alternative: Ask your students for stickers. They might have some that they are especially interested in.

In class

1. Show your students at least one sticker or hand out a copy of the sticker(s). Give your students a few minutes to talk about the sticker (or one of the stickers) in groups. The following questions might be helpful for their discussion:

    Where do you think this sticker was stuck when the teacher photographed it?
    What sort of person do you think put up this sticker? (Age, looks, job, interests, family background, life-style, political views, etc.)
    Imagine that there was a certain incident that made the person put up this sticker. What sort of incident do you think this was?

2. Imagine that the person who put up the sticker is having an argument (jokingly

or seriously) with someone about what the sticker says. What sort of person could this be? Write down their dialogue with your partner.

3. Collect all the dialogues. Hand them out so that each pair gets a dialogue written by another pair. Tell them that they are going to develop a role-play from this dialogue. Give them a few minutes to read the dialogues and ask questions if necessary. Then collect the dialogues again.

4. Give your class five minutes for each pair to develop a role-play out of the dialogue they have read. Tell them that they can either act out the dialogue as they remember it or change it in whatever way they like.

5. Ask your learners to act out their role-plays in class.

Sample stickers

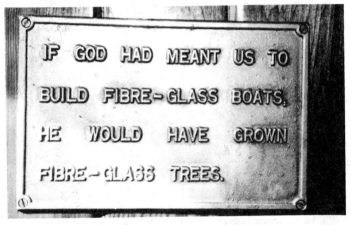

Don't drink and drive.
You might hit a bump
and spill your drink

Action research element

In an upper intermediate class in which the activity was tried out with the stickers presented above, one of the learners suggested that the class create their own slogans for stickers they would like to wear. We found this a very valuable suggestion. This learner based the slogan she created on one of the stickers from above. This is her slogan:

If God had meant us to build concrete houses, he would have grown concrete trees.

This learner has come up with a nice idea on how to drill *if*-clauses in an interesting way.

21 From picture to text

Types of picture:	Rough sketch on the board
Skill areas:	Speaking, listening, reading
Functions:	Reconstructing a text
Level:	Lower intermediate and above
Time:	20—30 minutes
Purpose:	Guessing a text with the help of first letters and reconstructing it

Preparation

The first letter of each word of a short text are written on the board, on an OHP transparency or on a sheet that is photocopied and handed out.

In class

1. Draw a rough sketch on the board featuring the essential elements of the text. Let your students guess what it is all about and help by giving hints to keep up the flow of the guesswork.

Sample drawing

2. Now show your learners the first letters of each word of the text and ask them to reconstruct it. Help by using gestures and mime, giving more letters, synonyms, definitions, etc. Do not, however, write anything into the gaps. When your learners can not go on try to help by reading out the text up to the word which they last managed to guess. The length of each word is roughly indicated by the length of the line following each first letter.

Sample text

P_____ p_____ o__ g_____
u_____ a_____ o____

f_____ a__ v_____. T____ o____ s__ a__ a__

q_____ s____ a__, 'H__ d__ y__ m_____ t__ g____ s____ b____

b_____ t_____?' etc.

Our garden

People passing our garden usually admire our flowers and vegetables. They often stop and ask questions such as, 'How do you manage to get such big, beautiful tomatoes?' Those questions make my father and my mother quite uneasy. They don't know what to say. What should they tell those people? Should they tell them that their daughter often goes out into the garden late at night, especially when there is a full moon? My parents don't know what I do out there. When I tell them that I'm going out into the garden they just give me a worried look and when I bend over the vegetables and flowers I sometimes see my parents' faces pressed against the windows. They are watching, but they never ask any questions. And I think it's better that way.

3. When they have finished reconstructing the text, ask them to write it down using the first letters as help.

   Alternative: Remove the first letters and have them write the text from memory. Ask them to compare their results with their neighbours'. Then get them to read out their texts and tell the others to interrupt when they think the original text was different.

22   Find the differences

Types of picture:	Any drawing, preferably with lots of details
Skill areas:	Speaking, listening
Grammar:	Questions and answers
Functions:	Asking for and giving information, language of description
Level:	Lower intermediate and above
Time:	15–20 minutes
Purpose:	Students discover differences between two pictures, ask and answer questions

Preparation

Select a drawing and photocopy it. Then use tippex, a pencil (felt pen) and scissors to make the copy different from the original in, say, twenty points (see the sample drawing below). Then copy the original and the drawing with the differences so that there are enough of each for half the number of students in your class.

In class

1. Get your students to work in pairs. Tell them that you are going to hand out a picture to each of them. Partner A and B in each pair will have different pictures. They should find out the differences without showing the drawings to each other.

2. Hand out the drawings and ask your learners to list the differences they have discovered.

Sample drawings

Picture 1

Solution to picture 1
The knot on the rope is missing.
The button hole on one lapel is missing.

Picture 2

Solution to picture 2

The pirate's left ear is missing.

The eyes on the parrot are different.

One bone on the hat is missing.

The blade of the knife is missing.

A feather on the crest of the parrot is missing.

The hair on the pirate's chest is missing.

One dot on the scarf is missing.

One stitch on the scar is missing.

The notch on the sword is missing.

One hook on the anchor is missing.

One button on the shoulder tab is missing.

23   From story to picture

Types of picture: Picture stories featuring stick-people

Skill areas: Reading, listening, speaking

Grammar: Past tense

Functions: Telling stories, correcting, agreeing, disagreeing

Level: Intermediate and above

Time: 60 minutes

Purpose: Practising the language of negotiation, telling stories from pictures

Preparation

You need copies of the texts of four stories plus two cartoons depicting the contents of two of the stories.

In class

1. Give copies of a story to half of the class and copies of a cartoon depicting the same story to the other half. Ask your learners to work in pairs. Partner A, who has got the text, reads the story silently and B, who has got the cartoon, tries to make up his/her mind what the picture story is all about. B then starts telling the story to A. A's task is to listen, to correct whenever necessary and to help with verbal prompts when B seems to be stuck or completely wrong concerning the content of the story.

    When B has finished telling the story, A reads it out. Then they change roles, using the text of another story and the cartoon depicting it.

2. The learners again work in pairs. But now both partners receive stories which they read. The stories are different and they are not allowed to show their texts to one another. Both partners then draw the contents of their stories in the form

of stick-people cartoons. When they have finished, A hands his cartoon to B, who tries to tell the story from the cartoon. A guides, helps and corrects if necessary. The roles are then changed.

Sample story and cartoon

The king and his two sons
Once upon a time there was a king who was a good man, and his people liked him very much. The king had two sons who both wanted to be the new king, since their father was old and tired of ruling his country. So the king asked his wise men, and they suggested giving each of his sons five gold coins. They should fill the great hall of the castle with what they could get for the five coins. Then it would be easy to decide who should be the next king. So the king called for his sons, gave them the

gold coins and told them their task. The young men immediately set out to win the crown. Soon the older son came to a big field. When he saw that there was lots of straw he had an idea. He offered the farmer his money if the farmer would fill the great hall of the castle with straw. The farmer was happy to be able to earn so much money, and during the next couple of days he filled the hall with straw. When he had finished, the old king shook hands with his older son since he had had such a good idea. Then the king's servants removed the straw to make the hall ready for the younger brother. The younger son had travelled through the country for several days, but he didn't know what to do with the money. One day he came to a market in a small town. There a girl was selling candles. The younger son talked to her, and after a while the girl asked him why he looked so unhappy. So the king's son told her that he had no idea how to fill the castle's hall. The girl smiled and asked him why he didn't fill the hall with light. He loved this idea and bought ten candles from her. Then he rode back to his father's castle. When he had lit all the candles and filled the hall with warm light, the wise men clapped their hands and the king handed his crown to his younger son. The first thing the young king did was to send for the girl he had bought the candles from. And, of course, he wanted to marry her. The girl, however, had brought her sister with her and so not only the young king got married but his brother too. And the young king gave half of his kingdom to his brother and his new wife.

Action research element

A group of students who were in their fourth year of learning English as a foreign language found it very useful to be offered some help when guiding and correcting their partners. The teacher wrote the following language exponents on the board:

> *There was/were more than/no . . .*
> *Before that happened there was something else.*
> *It was not only . . .*
> *It was just . . .*
> *No, he didn't . . . he . . .*
> *Not exactly, think of . . .*
> *Think of . . .*
> *But there was a problem*
> *What do you think happened before/after/ . . . ?*
> *It has got something to do with . . .*
> *Let me help you a bit.*
> *Was/Were/Did the . . . or . . . ?*
> *So who/when/what . . . ?*

24 Picture qu's

Types of picture:	Six to eight pictures, at least half of which should show some sort of action
Skill areas:	Speaking, listening
Vocabulary:	As related to content of picture
Grammar:	Past tense
Functions:	Narrating
Level:	Elementary and above
Time:	20–30 minutes
Purpose:	Enhancing your students' creativity, story telling

Preparation

Select a set of photographs as described above. Copy the photographs so that you have the same set of six to eight photos per group of four students for one half of your class. For each student of the other half prepare a photocopy of a worksheet containing comprehension questions in the past (e.g. *What happened after Little John had pushed Robin Hood into the river?*). There should be at least one question per picture, but the questions need not necessarily show a narrative link with one another.

In class

1. Divide your class in two halves and ask each half to work in groups of about four.

2. Give one set of pictures to each of the groups of the first half of the class. Ask them to create a story together based on the pictures.

3. Give the handouts with the comprehension questions to the groups belonging to the second half of your class. Ask each group to write a story together based on the comprehension questions.

4. Get each group to read out their story and compare the stories created.

Sample pictures

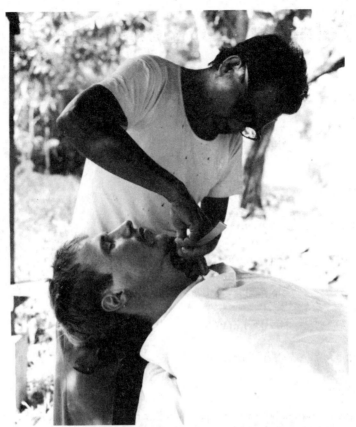

25 Telepathy or nonsense?

Types of picture:	Simple drawings of various objects on the board or wallpaper, or copies of drawings below
Skill areas:	Listening, speaking
Grammar:	*I think it's .../Is it ...?*
Functions:	Guessing an object
Level:	Elementary and above
Time:	10−15 minutes
Purpose:	Warm-up game

Preparation

Photocopy the drawings below or prepare similar ones on wallpaper (they could also easily be drawn on the board).

In class

1. Tell your students that you are going to do a little experiment with them. The aim of this experiment is to find out if telepathy works. Present the set of simple drawings of objects. Ask one student to leave the class for a minute.

2. Point to one of the pictures. Tell your students to communicate this picture to their colleague using mind power only as soon as s/he comes back into the classroom.

3. Ask the student back into class. The others concentrate on the picture chosen and try to 'tell' the student which picture has been selected.

4. After half a minute, ask the student who had left the class which picture s/he thinks the others wanted to communicate to him/her.

5. Repeat this procedure ten times (with different students). Note down the guesses on the board.

6. Send someone else out, decide on a picture, but this time get the students to concentrate deliberately on another picture. Repeat this ten times. Note all the guesses.

7. Compare the results together with your students. Ask them if they believe in telepathy. Some of them might like to tell mystery stories.

Sample drawings

26 Picture dictation

Types of picture:	Drawing or photo with lots of details (e.g. market scene)
Skill areas:	Listening, speaking
Grammar:	Prepositions
Functions:	Describing a picture, asking for location
Level:	Elementary and above
Time:	10–20 minutes
Purpose:	To enhance the students' listening skills, to get them to ask questions about details of a picture and to practise vocabulary

Preparation

Draw a picture (or select an appropriate photograph).

In class

1. Preteach vocabulary. For example, present all the necessary words that you think are new to your learners on poster paper or on the OHP. Give your class a minute to concentrate on the words. Ask them to work in pairs and to note down as many of the words as they can remember. Then get them to dictate the words back to you. Explain the meaning of the words by putting the words into a context, through mime and gesture, definitions, real objects, etc. Check that the students have understood the meaning of each word by asking them to give you sentences with the words.

2. If necessary, preteach language of reference. Do this by, for example, drawing a simple picture on the board and commenting while drawing, using the language below:

   In the centre of the picture there is ...

> *There is a ... in the background/foreground.*
> *On the right-/left-hand side of the ... there is ...*
> *In the top right/bottom left corner ...*
> *Close to the ... there is a (woman). She is ... ing ...*
> *Behind .../In front of .../Between the ... and the .../Next to the .../*
>   *Underneath the .../Above the ... there is/are ...*

3. Ask one learner to come to the front of the class. Give him/her the drawing or photograph. Tell the student to describe the picture to the class so that his/her classmates can draw the same picture without being shown the original.

4. Get your class to interrupt the student in front of the class and ask as many questions as necessary in order to draw a picture that comes as closely as possible to the original. If necessary, note down chunks of language on the board to assist your students with asking questions; for example:

> *Is there a ... in .../on .../next to the ... etc.*
> *Are there any ... etc.*
> *Is (the policeman) (looking) to the right/left etc.*
> *Has (he) got anything in (his) left/right hand etc.*
> *Is the ... bigger than the ...*
> *etc.*

5. After the picture dictation get your students to compare their drawings in pairs. Give them a few minutes to ask clarification questions. Then present the original (preferably on the OHP or enlarged on poster paper) for the students to compare.

27   A day in the life of . . .

Types of picture:	Pictures of people involved in doing their job, a hobby or a sport
Skill areas:	Speaking, listening, writing
Vocabulary:	Jobs, sports, hobbies
Grammar:	Present simple
Functions:	Describing habits
Level:	Intermediate and above
Time:	40 minutes
Purpose:	Creative writing

Preparation

Cut out pictures from magazines or newspapers as specified above.

In class

1. Show your learners a picture of a person involved in doing his/her job, a hobby or a sport; for example a scuba diver, then talk about a day in the life of a devoted scuba diver.

   Example:
   He gets up at six o'clock and takes a bath, trying out his new goggles in the bath tub. For breakfast he has fish and water, and then he goes out to shop for some new flippers. He hasn't got any in pink so that's what he's after. For lunch he has algae soup and then Frutta di Mare. In the afternoon he goes down to the beach and spends the afternoon under water. In the evening he sits in front of his fish tank watching the fish instead of TV. He sleeps on a water bed, of course.

   Alternative: You might write just the first letters of each word of a text you have prepared on the topic on the board and get your learners to reconstruct the text.

2. Now put several pictures up on the wall or hand out photocopies. Check whether your learners are familiar with the words and practise them if necessary. The learners work in pairs. They choose a picture and then write down their text: A day in the life of a devoted . . . .

3. The texts are then read out to the class.

28 Inner monologues

Types of picture: Portrait or photo of two people

Skill areas: Speaking, writing of inner monologues

Level: Intermediate and above

Time: 40–50 minutes

Purpose: Developing the learner's empathy with other people, creative writing

Preparation

Copy the sample photograph opposite or select an appropriate photo and produce as many copies as there are learners in your class. If it does not copy well, pin it on the wall or pass it round.

In class

1. Hand out the copies of the photographs. First get your learners to speculate about the picture. They should do this individually and should not share their speculations with their classmates. A few guiding questions might be helpful with this. For the sample picture these questions might be:

    Who do you think the people in the photo are?
    Where do you think the scene is taking place?
    What, in your opinion, is the relationship between the people in the photo?
    What do you think happened five minutes before?
    What do you think is going to happen in five minutes' time?

2. Get your learners to identify with one person or two of the people in the photograph. Ask them to write this person's inner monologue.

3. Correct your student's texts and get them to read them out aloud in class.

Sample picture

Action research element

It would be valuable for the teacher to draw up a list together with the students of things one should keep in mind when reading a text out aloud. These were the suggestions an upper intermediate class came up with:

Before reading a text out aloud:
Read through the text silently making sure you know how to pronounce the words.

While reading:
Speak clearly.
Do not speak too fast.
Make breaks so that your listeners can follow your ideas.
Have eye contact with your listeners.

29 Change the story

Preparation

Cut out pictures from magazines and newspapers as specified above.

In class

1. Stick the pictures on the wall and give your students sufficient time to look at them closely.

2. Tell a story and ask your learners to change it afterwards using at least three of the pictures presented. The learners should work individually or in pairs, make notes and tell the modified stories in class.

    Example (Skeleton story):
    Two very rich landlords, each owner of many race horses. A boasts about honesty of his best groom, B suggests bet: if groom is honest in any situation B will give A half of his horses, if groom is not honest A must give half of his horses. A accepts bet, B sends his beautiful daughter disguised as gypsy girl to A's manor house, B's daughter helps with work in stables, best groom falls in love with her. On day 'gypsy girl' is found lying in stable, very ill, says she is going to die very soon. Best groom wants to get doctor, girl says no, only help would be heart of best race horse, groom desperate but kills race horse, gives girl heart to eat,

78

girl recovers, next day girl gone. B visits A and tells him about incident, A sends for groom, asks how his best race horse is. Groom tells him that he killed best horse to save gypsy girl's life because he loves her. A very happy, gives him big reward.

Variation

The stories are told without endings. The students think of endings, then the teacher tells them the original one.

Action research element

When the students tell the modified stories, they show the listeners the pictures they have used to illustrate the changes they have made in the story.

One of the contributions was the following:

When the groom realised that the gypsy girl had gone, he fled (picture of plane). He went to live in a foreign country and found a job with a very rich widow (picture of woman) who also owned horses. He married her. After a couple of years they went abroad to watch a race. And there he met the 'gypsy girl' (picture of another woman), who told him that she was B's daughter and why she had deceived him although she had loved him too. She had also married, but was unhappy. So they decided to run away from their spouses. They met at night, but on their way to the airport they were both killed in an accident (picture of accident).

30 Tell an impromptu story

Types of picture:	Any, selected by the students (one by the teacher)
Skill areas:	Listening, story telling
Vocabulary:	As related to content of pictures
Grammar:	Past tense
Functions:	Narrating
Level:	Elementary and above
Time:	10—15 minutes
Purpose:	Telling impromptu stories. Developing listening skills; when the learners tell the stories, the activity is also aimed at developing long-turn talk.

Preparation

Ask your students to bring pictures of any kind to class (photos, pictures cut out from newspapers or magazines, etc.). They should not be too small (at least post-card size). Every student should bring at least fifteen pictures which they have glued on pieces of cardboard.

In class

1. Arrange your learners in a circle, each of them with their pictures. Tell them this:

    I am going to tell you a story. You can influence my story by holding up one of the pictures you have in front of you.
    Whenever you hold up a picture, I will try to integrate it into my story. Please hold up only one picture at a time.

2. Base the beginning of your story on the picture you have selected yourself. Hold

up the picture and start telling your story. In order to develop your learners' listening skills, gear the level of the story a bit above their language level.

Variation

Depending on the level of your class, you could ask a student to take over the role of story-teller from you.

Action research element

We have found that quite a lot of teachers expect this activity to be difficult to do. Once they tried it out, however, they commented that telling an impromptu story was fun and a lot less difficult than they had thought.

> NOTE: *This activity is based on an idea we got from Norman Skillen. For more ideas on story telling see J. Morgan and M. Rinvolucri,* Once Upon a Time *(Cambridge University Press, 1983).*

31 Changing a fairy tale

Types of picture:	Stick drawings
Skill areas:	Speaking, listening, writing
Grammar:	Past tense
Functions:	Narrating
Level:	Lower intermediate and above
Time:	40 minutes
Purpose:	Changing a well-known story in a creative way

Preparation

Stick-drawings of scenes depicting the beginnings and alternative endings of fairy tales.

In class

1. Draw the beginning of a well-known fairy tale on the board. If there are learners who do not know the fairy tale, ask a volunteer to tell it, or tell it yourself.

2. Then draw several endings on the board that are different from the traditional one. Ask your learners to guess what the drawings represent. Finally, sum up each ending and ask your students to think of what has happened between the beginning and one of the alternative endings. Ask them to work in pairs, to make notes and then tell their version or to write down the story and read it out.

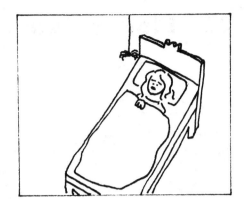

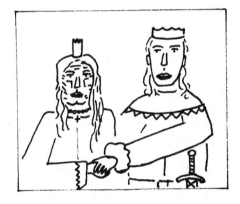

32 Flow of words

Types of picture:	Any, preferably without people, e.g. an object, a still life, a room, etc.
Skill area:	Creative writing
Level:	Lower intermediate and above
Time:	20–30 minutes
Purpose:	To help students overcome writing blocks and develop their creativity

Preparation

Make one copy for each student of the sample picture below or a similar photograph from a newspaper or magazine.

In class

1. Tell your class about a student you once had who found it extremely difficult to write texts in English. The problem for this student was that he was so critical of his own work that he never got over the hurdle of the first sentence. Tell them that you helped this person to overcome his writing block by telling him to write a bad first sentence knowing that he could always correct it later or substitute a better one for it. This helped him to get into the flow of writing without judging his own work at such an early stage. Later he found it easy to correct and improve his own texts. Tell them that the activity they are going to do is aimed at helping people to overcome writing blocks and to get into a creative flow of writing.

2. Hand out a copy of the photograph to each student. Give them a minute to look at it. They should then write for five minutes. Their text could be a story, a description, an inner monologue, or a poem without rhyme. Tell them that they should 'send their inner watch dog away'. That means that they should not judge their texts while they are writing them. They should also not try hard to avoid making errors, or to structure their texts in paragraphs, but just allow a 'flow of words'. Tell them that it is important that they do not pause at all.

3. Pair up your learners and get them to help each other with the correction of the texts. The texts can be either read out or put up on a wall for everybody in class to read.

Sample photograph

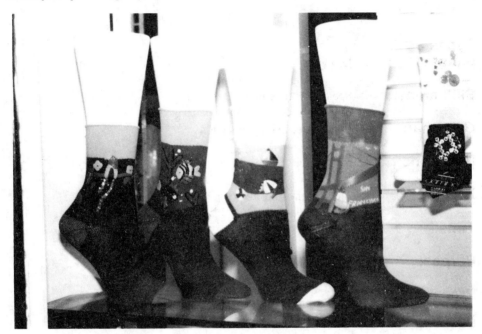

Action research element

Classroom experience has shown that this technique resulted in texts of considerable poetic value. Students were surprised about the quality (and also quantity) of what they produced within such a short period of time.

33   I'll always remember that

Types of picture:	Drawing
Skill areas:	Speaking, listening, note taking
Grammar:	Past tense, asking questions
Functions:	Narrating
Level:	Elementary and above
Time:	50 minutes
Purpose:	To stimulate sharing of past experiences

Preparation

None.

In class

1. Make a drawing on the board that shows a childhood experience that you remember very well, and tell your learners about it.

    Example:

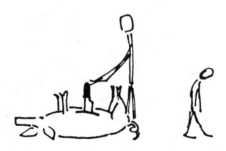

When I was very small I once watched a butcher slaughter a pig. Everything was full of blood and I felt very sick. And for years I refused to eat meat.

In order to avoid making your learners think only of negative incidents make another drawing that represents a positive experience from your past.

2.   Ask your learners to think back to their childhood and to remember an interesting situation. Tell them to make a simple drawing. Then ask them to get into groups of five, show their drawings and tell their stories.

3.   When they have finished, ask your learners to think of another situation and make a drawing. They then show their drawings and the others in the group start guessing what they are all about. The one whose drawing is being talked about clarifies and adds information if necessary.

NOTE: *We got the idea for this activity from* Poem into Poem *by Alan Maley and Sandra Moulding (Cambridge University Press, 1985).*

---

34 Create your story

Types of picture:	At least 20 pictures, taken at random from magazines, newspapers, etc.
Skill area:	Creative writing
Grammar:	Past tense
Function:	Narrating
Level:	Lower intermediate and above
Time:	40–50 minutes
Purpose:	To develop the students' ability to narrate and take part in long-turn talk

Preparation

Collect photographs from magazines. They should not be related to each other, but be likely to stimulate the interest of the students.

In class

1. Stick all the pictures on the wall. Ask your students to walk round and select individually (or in pairs) six pictures without removing them from the wall.

2. Put up large sheets of poster paper underneath the pictures. Ask your learners to write down legibly under the photos words that come to their minds when they look at their photographs. If they do not know a word in English, supply them with dictionaries or get them to ask you for the words they need.

3. Hand out a copy of the following sentences (or create your own sentences depending on the level of your class and the pictures you have chosen). Ask your students to select one of the sentences and write a story (individually or in pairs) based on their six pictures. The sentence they have chosen should be the last sentence in their story. Before they start writing, they should take time to look at their pictures and the words underneath.

The old man turned round, then he smiled, shut the door of the house and slowly disappeared into the dark forest.

Nobody saw the woman again and everybody was glad she had left.

'Now I can buy a new one', Tony said and laughed.

She felt the thing in her pocket and she knew that she was safe now.

If he had known that, he would never have returned to the places of his childhood.

The young girl smiled and, to his surprise, she reached into her bag and gave him the photo.

They all looked at him, but nobody recognised him.

4. Sit your class in a semi-circle facing the wall with the pictures. Ask each student (pair) to read out their text. Get the other learners to speculate about the six pictures that each author (pair) used as a basis for their text.

Variations

1. Present a set of sentences and ask your learners to use one of these as the beginning of their story.

2. Present two different sets of sentences. Ask your learners to select a beginning and an ending.

35 Old people

Types of picture:	A photo, painting or drawing of an old woman or man
Skill areas:	Speaking, listening, writing
Function:	Speculating about the past
Level:	Lower intermediate and above
Time:	60 minutes
Purpose:	Sharing opinions, creative writing

Preparation

Cut out a photo of an old man or woman and photocopy it for each student in your class, or cut out several photos so that there is one photo for each group of three or four.

In class

1. Hand out photocopies of the photo or hand the photos around. Tell your learners how old the person/the people in the photo(s) is/are. Then ask them to work in pairs and to note down what they think life was like when the person in the photo was their age. Ask them to consider the following topics and write the following language exponents on the board.

    Topics: school, holidays, work, spare time, pocket money, relationships, dating, fashion, traffic, travelling, sports, presents, housing, meals etc.

    Language exponents:
    We think there were a lot of/some/no/fewer/only a few/hardly any/...
    We suppose there was a/a lot of/some
    We don't suppose there was any ...
    The woman/man probably used to ...
    As far as ... is concerned ... they certainly didn't/had to/could/couldn't ...

2. Ask your learners to pool their notes with another pair. Then a secretary from

each group sums up the ideas and reports to the class. The most important ideas are taken down on poster paper (board) by the teacher or a class secretary.

3. Assign your learners the task of interviewing real people of roughly the same age as the person in the photo you handed out.

    In the next class: ask your students to report on what they found out. Compare their findings with the ideas on the poster paper (board) from the previous lesson.

4. Hand out the photo again and tell them to write down one piece of advice on a sheet of paper which the old person would consider important to convey to young people. They should not write their names on the sheets of paper. Then ask your students to imagine for a moment that they are the old person. Give them a minute to 'feel' what it is like to be such an old person.

    Collect the pieces of paper and read them out. After reading each one, get your students to discuss whether or not they consider the piece of advice to be useful for themselves.

Sample photo

36 Childhood memories

Types of picture:	Photos of the students taken when they were children
Skill areas:	Writing, reading, listening, speaking
Grammar:	*I used to ...*
Functions:	Narrating childhood events
Level:	Lower intermediate and above
Time:	50 minutes
Purpose:	Students write poems based on childhood photos, talk about the poems and their childhood memories

Preparation

Ask each student to bring to class a photo taken when s/he was a child. Ask them to put this photo in an envelope and seal it. They should not write their names on the envelope.

In class

1. Tell your students a pleasant episode from your childhood; for example:
   When I was about six or seven, my parents and I often went to a small mountain village for a holiday. We often went to a pleasant brook there and I remember building dams with stones and boats from bark ...

2. Ask your learners to think of a happy time in their childhood. Write 'I used to ...' on the board and tell them to give you a sentence relating to this time.

   Examples:

   > *I used to go hiking with my father a lot.*
   > *I used to help my gran in the garden.*
   > *I used to drive a tractor when I was only ten.*
   > *I used to listen to my gran telling stories.*

Ask them to give you a sentence each and correct it if necessary. When everybody has said their sentence, ask them to choose the sentence they liked best (not their own) and to say it aloud.

3. Present the text below on the OHP (or on strips of paper) in the following way. Your students see only one line at a time, very briefly, and try to write it down. Allow some time for the writing. First they see just the first line for a few seconds, then the second line, etc. When they have finished writing down the text, they can check with their neighbour and correct their text if necessary. Two or three students then read out their texts and you show them the text on the OHP for final correction.

> *I used to dream of expensive clothes*
> *I used to dream of a holiday in Hawaii*
> *I used to dream of a Porsche*
> *and of parties under a silvery moon*
> *but all I want right now*
> *is a friend*
> *who will listen to me.*

4. Ask your learners to mark their envelopes with a symbol, such as a cross, a flower, etc. Collect the envelopes with the childhood pictures. Hand them out so that no one gets their own envelope. Ask them to open the envelopes, look at the pictures for a time and then create a text, based on the picture and the following prompts, which you write on the board:

> *S/he used to dream of* _____
> *S/he used to dream of* _____
> *S/he used to dream of* _____
> *and of* _____
> *but all s/he wants right now*
> *is* _____
> _____

5. Collect the photos and texts. While you are putting up the photos and the texts on the board, ask the students to write a text for themselves (based on the same prompts as above, but starting with 'I used to . . .' and put it next to their childhood photograph and the text created by someone else.

6. Students walk round and read as many texts as possible.

NOTE: This is an adaptation of an activity from our book on practising grammar structures by drawing on resources from both hemispheres of the brain. Source: G. Gerngross and H. Puchta, Creative Grammar *(Pilgrims—Longman Resource Books, 1992).*

37   Who lives behind that door?

Types of picture: Several photos of doors

Skill area: Listening, speaking and writing

Functions: Describing people, narrating

Level: Intermediate and above

Purpose: Developing short turn talk, creative writing

Preparation

Photocopy the sample pictures or cut out photos of doors from magazines.

In class

1.   Hand out photocopies of several doors or stick them up on the wall. Ask your students to write down (notes) a description of a person they think might be living behind one of the doors. The description should include: age, marital status, family, appearance, characteristics, hobbies, likes and dislikes, lifestyle, job, interior of the house or flat.

2.   Get the students to form groups of four to six according to the door they have chosen. They each present their personalities to the group. Each group finally decides on one description they like best. Each member copies the notes concerning the description they have chosen and then other suitable ideas from other descriptions are added.

3.   Each student now looks for a partner (A, B) from a group that has chosen another door. A starts speculating about the person living behind B's door. When A has finished, B reads out the description they have worked on in step 2. Then they change roles: B speculates about the person living behind A's door and then A reads out his/her description.

Variations

(a) Interviewing a door: Half of the class receive pictures of doors. The second half writes down questions they could ask when interviewing a door, for example 'How long have you been working here? Are you satisfied with your job/your owners? Is there a lot of noise in the street? Are the nights quiet?' etc. Then the interviews are held. When this step takes place in groups, one interview in each group is chosen to be presented to the whole class later on.

(b) The students write a story, 'A dramatic moment in the life of a door', using one of the following sentences as an ending:

- *When s/he finally slammed me in her/his face I knew that they would never talk to each other again.*
- *After that the dog never used me as a toilet again.*
- *They finally had a new lock put in.*

(c) Instead of doors, pictures of windows could be used for steps 1–3.

38 Bridges

Types of picture:	A photo or painting of a bridge
Skill areas:	Creative writing, listening, speaking, reading aloud
Function:	Narrating
Level:	Intermediate and above
Time:	15–20 minutes in the first lesson, 20–30 minutes in the second lesson
Purpose:	Creative writing, story telling, listening

Preparation

Copy Monet's *The Water Lily Pond* (or any other picture of a bridge) for half the number of your students.

In class

First lesson

1. In a quiet and calm voice ask your students to close their eyes. Ask them to think of a bridge. Give them time. Then continue:

    As you are sitting there trying to think of a bridge ... I have no idea what bridge you are thinking of ... where it is situated ... maybe it is in the middle of a big city ... or somewhere in a little village in the country ... or somewhere completely different ... maybe there is a big river, a lively little brook, or a motorway below the bridge you are thinking of ... and thinking of this bridge might bring back memories ... memories of towns, or landscapes, or memories of people ... or any other memories ... maybe you can see some images, clear or vague, maybe you can hear sounds or voices ... or maybe also recall feelings while you see and hear something ... and for some of us a bridge might also be a symbol ... maybe of two things you want to bring together, you want to connect ... or you may think of a decision you have to make ... whatever comes

to your mind now ... it is okay ... allow yourself to have all these memories
and thoughts and pictures and feelings ... and take the time you need until you
want to come back to this classroom again ... and when you feel it is right for
you ... open your eyes again ... and stretch a little.

2. Get your students to work in pairs. Hand out a copy of Monet's *Water Lily Pond*
    or any other picture of a bridge to each pair. Get the students to compare the
    bridge in the painting and the bridge they were thinking of in the guided fantasy.
    Then ask them to tell stories in which a bridge they remember plays a role.

Second lesson
1. Ask your students to close their eyes again and think of the bridge they saw in
    the guided fantasy of the previous lesson. They should also think of the bridge
    stories they heard. Then ask them to write a short, reflective text based on their
    thoughts and memories. It should be about six to eight sentences long, need not
    have a real ending or beginning, could sketch a mood, a glimpse of a thought,
    an insight, a feeling or the like. If necessary, read out to the students one or two
    models.

2. Students read out their texts in class. Encourage them to comment on their
    classmates' texts, ask questions, etc.

Sample picture

Action research element

Comparing Monet's painting of the bridge with the bridges from their fantasies triggered off lots of stories with the students in our trial classes. The most interesting one, perhaps, was a woman's story about giving birth to her daughter in an ambulance in Graz while it was crossing a bridge.

> NOTE: *This activity is based on a similar exercise with pictures of walls which we got from David A. Hill at Pilgrims in Canterbury. His book* Visual Impact (Longman, 1989) offers lots of ideas.

39 Who's the driver?

Types of picture:	Several pictures of cars
Skill areas:	Listening and speaking
Functions:	Describing people, giving reasons
Level:	Intermediate and above
Time:	40 minutes
Purpose:	Developing short-turn talk, making notes

Preparation

Photocopies of different cars or clippings from magazines. Car magazines are a rich source for such photos. There should be at least three different pictures of cars. The pictures are either stuck on the wall or photocopies are handed out to each student.

In class

1. Ask your learners to work in groups of three to five. Tell them to make notes of at least three reasons why they would like to own a certain car.

2. Write 'I'd like to have a ... because ...' on the board. Tell your learners to use this structure when giving their reasons. If the learner already owns the car of his/her choice, ask him/her to use: 'I bought this car because ...' as a starter. If a learner does not want to own any car at all, ask him/her to use: 'I wouldn't like to have any kind of car, because ...' as a starter.

3. Hand out photocopies of cars or stick pictures/photocopies on the wall. Ask your students to pick one car and to make notes concerning a person they think might own such a car (person's appearance, age, marital status, job, hobbies, likes and dislikes).

4. Ask your students to form groups according to the cars they have chosen. If there are more than five learners in any group, have them form two or more groups

using the same car as stimulus. Get them to talk about the person they think owns a certain car.

Alternative: Instead of making notes, the students write down descriptions of the people and stick them on the wall next to the respective car. Ask them to read as many descriptions as possible.

Variation

The same steps could be used with pictures of houses, rooms, paintings, dogs.

40 Guessing landscapes

Types of picture:	Views of open countryside
Skill areas:	Speaking, listening
Vocabulary:	Relating to landscape, scenery
Grammar:	*Is there ...?, Are there ...?*, prepositions
Functions:	Asking questions
Level:	Intermediate and above
Time:	20 minutes
Purpose:	To introduce and practise vocabulary, to stimulate visualisation

Preparation

Cut out pictures from holiday brochures, magazines or newspapers.

In class

1. Use several pictures to teach the following words: *view, scene, scenery, island, sea, ocean, lake, loch, lagoon, bay, fjord, wave, roller, shore, beach, surf, river, stream, brook, waterfall, canal, bank, hill, mountain, slope, summit, cliff, cave, valley, plain, moor, swamp, desert, forest, wood, jungle, clearing, volcano.*

2. Use several techniques to practise the words; for example, ask your learners to call out the words when you flash the pictures. Do the same with flashcards on which the words have been written down. Put all the pictures on the board (wall) using blu-tack. Ask your learners to close their eyes. Remove five to seven pictures. Tell them to open their eyes, and ask, 'Which pictures are missing?' Write the first letters of the words on the board and ask your students to call them out aloud.

3. Ask a student to take one picture from the pile you have used without showing it to you. Guess the picture by asking questions to which the student can answer 'Yes' or 'No'. Tell the student to show the picture when he/she thinks that you have come very close.

4. Ask your students to work in pairs. Hand out one picture to each student and tell them not to show it to their partners. One in each pair starts guessing his/her partner's picture. When the essential features have been correctly guessed, the pictures should be shown. Then the partners change roles. To make the task easier, the students whose pictures are being guessed may, of course, help a little by saying things like: 'No, it's not actually a river, but . . .' 'You are very close', 'There's something in the forest you haven't guessed yet', etc.

5. When a pair has finished, they swap pictures with another pair.

41 Ask the teacher questions

Types of picture:	Photos of the teacher in various situations
Skill areas:	Listening, speaking, writing
Grammar:	Practising questions
Functions:	Asking for information, comparing answers given by the teacher with expected answers, sharing information, sharing opinions
Level:	Intermediate and above
Time:	30–40 minutes
Purpose:	Students get to know their teacher better, the teacher gets some feedback on how s/he is perceived by his/her students

Preparation

Select five to ten pictures showing you in various situations in different phases of your life.

In class

1. Briefly tell your class that you have brought along some photos showing yourself at various stages in your life. Display all the photos so that your students can easily see them. Put them on the floor in the middle of a circle of chairs, allow students to pick photos up and hand them round, or stick all the photos on the wall and have the students stand up and look at the photographs.

2. Tell the students that you are going to answer questions. Get them to think of questions they would like to ask you based on the photographs. These questions could be directly linked to photographs (*Who is the person with you in this picture?*) or could also be more general (*Did you smoke when you were a teenager?*) Ask them to note their questions down.

3. Play some soft, meditative music. Get students to close their eyes and *imagine* that they are asking you their questions. Ask them to *imagine* that you are actually going to answer their questions too. Get them to take notes of the answers they receive in the imaginary interview.

4. Now ask them to read out their questions one by one, and answer them.

5. Get each student to talk about the answers they had expected and the ones you gave. Depending on the size of the class this could also be done in groups.

Variation

Instead of getting the students to image the teacher's answers, you can also have your class sitting in a horseshoe arrangement with you as the focus. One student sits on your right and one on your left, and answers the questions for you.

NOTE: *We have taken this the activity from J. Canfield and H.C. Wells* 100 Ways to Enhance Self-concept in the Classroom *(Prentice Hall Curriculum and Teaching Series, 1976). Tessa Woodward presents various variations of this activity in her book* Recipes for Teacher Training *(Pilgrims—Longman, 1992).*

42 Holiday pictures

Types of picture:	Pictures of tourist resorts
Skill areas:	Speaking, listening, writing, reading
Vocabulary:	Language of holiday brochures
Functions:	Giving reasons, making complaints, creative writing
Level:	Intermediate and above
Time:	40 minutes
Purpose:	Developing a critical attitude towards the language of adverts, writing a letter of complaint, letter writing

Preparation

Cut out pictures of resorts from holiday brochures. Write down words and phrases used in the brochures to advertise holiday resorts.

In class

1. The teacher shows the pictures taken from holiday brochures and asks the students where they would like to spend their holidays and why they would like to spend them there. Give them several minutes to make notes. If the group is fairly large, get two or three students to talk about their choice of place and the reasons why they would like to go there, in order to establish a model for the discussion. Then have them work in two or three groups of eight to ten.

2. The teacher writes words/chunks of language on the board (OHP) or hands out a worksheet. S/he explains that the words and chunks are examples of the notoriously exaggerated language travel agents sometimes use. The students should find out what is really meant by those words and phrases.

    Examples: carnival atmosphere, proud natives, unspoilt and quiet, simply furnished, cosy rooms, sundrenched, mild and pleasant weather, internationally known resort, glorious holiday playground, etc.

> *carnival atmosphere — noisy day and night*
> *proud natives — unfriendly natives*
> *sundrenched — very hot*
> *internationally known resort — crowded*
> *glorious holiday playground — overdeveloped*
> etc.

3. The teacher hands out pictures from holiday brochures. The students work in groups of four. One pair writes an exaggerated advert about the place shown in the picture, the other pair writes a letter of complaint from a person who has stayed in the same place. Depending on the level, you might want to give an example of an advert text and a letter of complaint.

4. The pictures and texts are then displayed on the walls of the classroom. The students are asked to mill around and to read as many texts as possible.

43 Rogerian listening

Types of picture:	Photo from newspaper or magazine that is likely to trigger off controversial opinions
Skill areas:	Speaking, listening
Functions:	Language of argumentation, agreeing, disagreeing
Level:	Advanced
Time:	20–30 minutes
Purpose:	Awareness training for listening, practising discussion

Preparation

Select a photo from a newspaper or magazine that is likely to trigger off controversial discussion. Place this photograph in the middle of an A4 sheet of paper. Around the photograph draw speech bubbles containing quotations that you think will stimulate discussion.

Alternative: If the photograph you have selected is larger (e.g. poster size) the speech bubbles could be cut out and stuck on the blackboard with the photograph in the middle.

In class

1. Hand out one copy of the photograph per student and give them five minutes or so to prepare for a discussion. Tell your students that they should look at the picture and consider carefully the opinions expressed in the speech bubbles. Then they should make notes concerning their own opinions.

2. Get your students to work in threes.

3. Tell your students that you want Student A and B in each group to discuss their opinion in a Rogerian listening style. This means that A first states his/her opinion. B listens attentively and before making his/her point has to repeat what he/she thinks A has said. If A does not agree with what B thinks A's point was, B tries again. If A agrees, B goes on to state his/her own opinion, and before A gives

an answer has to repeat what s/he thinks B has said. That means that A and B always sum up what they think their partner has said before they go on. It is C's role to observe the process and to see that the rules are kept.

4. After a quarter of an hour, interrupt the discussions and get your students to reflect on the process they have just experienced or observed. The following questions might facilitate this:

> *What did I find easy/difficult about the activity?*
> *What did I notice about myself/my partner(s)?*
> *What have I learnt through the activity about my own/other people's behaviour in discussions?*

Sample picture

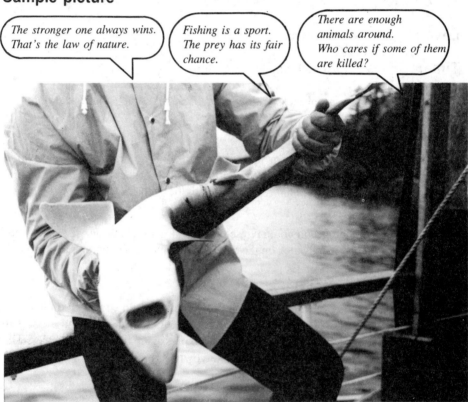

Action research element

This activity has proven very powerful and has been regarded as an eye opener by some learners in the groups we have tried it with. The following comment made by an adult advanced learner may illustrate this:

> For me this was a fascinating exercise. I always thought that I was a really good listener and I have now learnt that it is so easy to get your partner wrong. Sometimes I feel that we do not really try to comprehend what somebody is saying, but just hear what we expect we are going to hear. No wonder that we so often get frustrated about failure in communication. I think what we need to learn in order to be able to communicate better with each other is to listen better.

44 Worries

Types of picture:	Pictures or drawings of people doing perfectly ordinary things such as skiing, sitting on a train (plane, etc.) eating in a restaurant, having a picnic, swimming in a public pool, watching a performance at a theatre, etc.
Skill areas:	Speaking, listening, writing
Grammar:	*could, might*
Function:	Giving reasons
Level:	Lower intermediate and above
Time:	20 minutes
Purpose:	Finding and giving reasons, enhancing creativity

Preparation

Cut out pictures from magazines or newspapers as specified above or prepare stick-people drawings.

In class

1. Show your learners a picture (e.g. people sitting in a plane). Ask them to imagine how many reasons a worrier could find for not flying. Offer one or two examples and then give them time to make notes. Then elicit several more ideas from the class.

   Examples:
   The pilot might have forgotten to put on his contact lenses, a passenger could open the wrong door when trying to go to the toilet, a fight could break out among the passengers if the flight attendants run out of one of the dishes offered in the menu, etc.

2. Now show another picture (drawing) of people doing something perfectly ordinary, or hand out photocopies. Your learners work in groups of three or four. Tell them

to put themselves into the shoes of an extreme worrier. Their task is to write down reasons such a person could think of for not doing the activity shown in the picture. The teams then present their ideas by reading them out.

Variation

Different groups work on different pictures.

45 A picture interview

Types of picture:	Photo of a well-known person (contemporary or historical)
Skill areas:	Speaking, listening
Grammar:	Questions
Functions:	Asking for information, asking for opinions, giving information, giving opinions
Level:	Intermediate and above
Time:	15–20 minutes
Purpose:	Students practise asking questions

Preparation

Select a portrait photo large enough for everyone in class to see.

In class

1. Place the photo on the board or wall in front of the class. If the photo is not big enough, pass it round for everybody to look at. Tell your learners that they should note down questions they would like to ask this person if the person was actually present in the classroom.

2. Ask one learner to come to the front and, holding the VIP's picture in his/her hands, identify with the VIP. Ask this learner to answer the class's questions as the person in the portrait.

> NOTE: *We learnt this activity from Mario Rinvolucri. See J. Morgan and M. Rinvolucri* The Q Book *(Longman 1988), for further ideas.*

46 Pretty woman/Handsome man

Types of picture:	Pictures focusing on a pretty woman or a handsome man
Skill areas:	Speaking, listening, writing
Function:	Dialogue writing
Level:	Intermediate and above
Time:	50 minutes
Purpose:	Writing dialogues and monologues

Preparation

Cut out pictures as specified above from magazines or newspapers.

In class

1. Show the class a picture of an attractive man or woman and ask them to imagine a situation in which some sort of interaction takes place. The partner in this interaction should be of the opposite sex.

   Examples:

   > *Imagine the person is in a public swimming pool. S/he is just buying some ice-cream.*
   > *Imagine the person is dancing with someone at a party.*
   > *Imagine the person is a shop assistant, or flight attendant. S/he is just talking to a customer.*
   > *Imagine the person is doing some shopping in town. A stranger asks the way to the post office.*

   If the picture, however, clearly suggests a certain situation, no example needs to be given.

2. Ask your learners to work in pairs and give them four different writing tasks. Thus — depending on the size of the group — several pairs may do the same task.

Number 1:   What goes on in the person's mind? Write an interior monologue.

Number 2:   What goes on in the head of the peson who interacts with him or her? Write an interior monologue.

Number 3:   Two middle-aged men are talking about the woman. Write down their dialogue. Two middle-aged women are watching the man. Write down their dialogue.

The students write in pairs and then read out their texts.

47 Filling speech bubbles

Types of picture:	Copies of cartoons from newspapers, parts of photo-romances, etc.
Skill areas:	Writing, reading
Grammar:	Direct speech
Level:	Lower intermediate and above
Time:	20–30 minutes
Purpose:	Developing short-turn talk, creative writing; students interpret scenes out of cartoons or photo-romances and write a dialogue

Preparation

Cut out or copy a cartoon or a situation from a photo-romance. Tippex out the words and sentences in the speech bubbles. Depending on the level of your class, you might want to leave some words in the bubbles as stimuli.

In class

1. Ask your learners to work in pairs or small groups. Hand out copies of the cartoon or parts of a photo-romance. Get your learners to talk about the situation. Write down a few guiding questions if necessary, for example:

    What do you think is going on in the scene?
    Who are the people?
    What is their relationship to each other?
    What do you think the people in the photos/drawings are talking about?

2. Get your learners to fill in the speech bubbles. Ask them to do this legibly. If the bubbles do not provide enough space, get your learners to write on an extra sheet of paper.

3. Have your students read out their ideas.

4. Hand out another cartoon/photo-romance or photocopies of it. This time do not remove the content of the speech bubbles. Ask the students (again in pairs) to write a narrative account. Get your students to write an ending (a beginning) that is different from the one in the pictures/photos.

48 Ads

Types of picture:	Advertisements
Skill areas:	Speaking, listening, writing
Grammar:	Word order
Function:	Language of advertising
Level:	Intermediate and above
Time:	40 minutes
Purpose:	Creative writing

Preparation

Cut out lots of ads from magazines, but remove the texts or captions that go with them.

In class

1. Present an ad or a photocopy of it. Write the slogan that goes with it on the board, but in jumbled order. Ask your class to reconstruct it. Example (the picture shows a man in mountain-climbing gear on top of a very high peak covered in snow): *you/you/your/first/get/drive/the/when/its/feeling/Porsche.*

    The solution was: *It's the feeling you get when you drive your first Porsche.*

    Alternative: Stick several pictures of ads on the walls of your classroom and write the captions — in jumbled word order — on the board (OHP). Ask them to put them right and to decide which ad goes with which caption.

2. Present an ad (several ads) and ask your learners to write captions in pairs. The captions are then read out and the best one is put beneath the ad. Finally, the original caption is read out by the teacher.

3. Show the picture of an advertisement *and* the caption. Ask your students to write alternative captions. These are then read out.

Action research element

An example of step 2 by students in their fourth year of English as a foreign language (the advert shows two small children in raincoats under a grey sky on a deserted beach in front of a closed Punch and Judy booth): the original caption read *At least 'Kodacolor' Gold Film performed*; one of the captions written by students ran *Sorry, Punch and Judy have moved their headquarters to Majorca*.

An example of step 3 by students in their third year (the advert shows a girl in jeans, blouse and pullover on a deserted beach; she seems to be doing a stretching exercise); the caption was *Women sweat, too*. It was an ad for a deodorant. Some captions produced by learners were: *Why didn't I buy a Donna bikini? I don't think I've got the right jogging shoes. A cigarette would make all the difference.*

49   Feelings

Types of picture:	Magazine pictures or photographs showing people in situations with a strong emotional impact
Skill areas:	Listening, speaking, writing
Vocabulary:	Words to do with feelings
Grammar:	. . . *because*
Function:	Giving reasons
Level:	Lower intermediate and above
Time:	40 minutes
Purpose:	Students talk about their own and other people's emotions

Preparation

Select photographs or magazine pictures as described above (five to ten).

In class

1. Present a display of the photos and pictures you have selected. Arrange them in a pattern similar to the one in the drawing below.

2. Ask your class to work in groups of three. Each group selects one photo. They discuss the picture (Who is the person? What sort of situation is s/he in? What other people not visible in the picture could be involved in the situation? etc.) and try to agree on the feelings of the person or people shown in the picture.

3. When the groups have finished their discussions, ask group secretaries to go to the board and write the emotive words along rays of chalk or felt tip shooting out from the centre towards the pictures. Next to the pictures themselves they should write the reasons why the people in the pictures might be experiencing these feelings. This should be done in keywords only, not in full sentences.

119

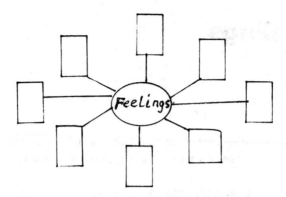

4. Give the class a few minutes to come to the board and have a close look at the pictures and at what their classmates have written down. Focus on each picture. For each picture in turn, read out the feelings associated with the picture and the reasons given for them. Ask the students if they agree/disagree with the suggestions made or if they want to make further suggestions themselves.

5. Ask your learners each to choose one of the emotive words on the 'rays' and think of a situation in which they themselves or someone they know had this feeling. Get them either to talk (in groups of not more than six to eight students) about this situation or to write a narrative text about it.

> NOTE: *This activity is part of a project on how to establish a link between the students' own feelings about the world and the reality of the language class. For more detailed information see H. Puchta and M. Schratz* Teaching Teenagers *(Pilgrims–Longman 1992).*

50 Death

Types of picture: Dead people, animals, plants

Skill areas: Speaking, listening, writing

Function: Creative writing

Level: Advanced

Time: 50 minutes

Purpose: Poetry writing

Preparation

Bring pictures as specified above or photocopy the sample pictures below.

In class

1. Give your learners enough time to look at the pictures. You might play a piece of solemn music.

2. Write the word 'Death' on the board and ask them to write down as many words as possible that they associate with it. Then ask them for their words and write them all on the board. If an association is not obvious, ask for the context: 'What do you mean by ...? How is that connected with/related to ...'

3. Now ask your learners to write a haiku with the title 'Death'. Remind them that haikus originated in Japan and that a haiku has three lines of five, seven and five syllables. The lines do not rhyme. Read out the example below twice. Then ask them to choose one of the pictures (dead person, animal, plant) and to write their haiku.

> *A moment ago*
> *I envied its graceful flight*
> *its loss ages me*

Variation

The students choose one of the pictures and write a story whose theme is 'loss'. The stories are then read out in class or shared in smaller, more personal and supportive groups.

Sample pictures

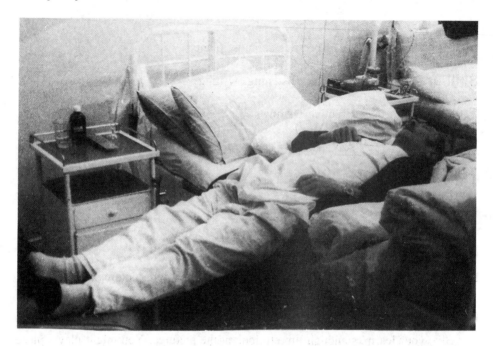

51 Computer games

Types of picture:	Cover picture of computer game
Function:	Writing a description of a computer game
Level:	Intermediate and above
Time:	20–30 minutes
Purpose:	Students write a description of computer game based on some model texts

Preparation

Photocopies of the descriptions and the cover picture below. Alternatively, select the cover of a computer program that is likely to inspire writing.

In class

1. Hand out a copy of the following descriptions of computer games and ask your students to read them:

   TUG-OF-WAR
   Program type: Two-player Arcade
   This game has you battling in a rather friendly situation. Each team must attempt to pull the other by pressing the appropriate key when the 'pull sign' lights. The first to hit his key gains the advantage, but if you are too quick, the team will slip and fall.

   FAST FOOD LASER
   Program type: Shoot-'m-up
   Set in a lonely burger bar in the depths of nowhere, a sole laser gun battles with a selection of fearsome fast food. Ketchup has become radioactive, normal food has been transformed into bloodthirsty monsters.
   *   You control a laser gun near the cafe where the sadistic snacks are. Your task is to save the world from destruction by preventing the enraged eats escaping.*

SORCERER'S QUEST
Program type: Text adventure
You are a fearless knight and have to destroy an evil sorcerer who is completely crazy. For your fight you must find three magical objects — a cup, a sword, and a shield.

2. Hand out a copy of the cover picture below or show your learners one that you have selected. Get them to create their own descriptions of a computer game (for one of the following program types: Arcade/Simulation/Logic game/Text adventure/Shoot-'m-up) individually or in pairs for the copy/picture you have shown to them. Ask them also to think of a catchy title.

Sample cover picture

NOTE: *We got the idea for this activity from Christian Holzmann.*

---

52 A woman and a man

Types of picture:	Pictures that focus on a man and a woman
Skill areas:	Speaking, listening, writing
Functions:	Creative writing
Level:	Intermediate and above
Time:	60 minutes
Purpose:	To practise dialogue writing

Preparation

Cut out pictures from magazines or newspapers as specified above.

In class

If possible pair your learners in such a way that a woman and a man (boy/girl) work together. Hand out the pictures or copies of one picture. Ask your learners to imagine that the people in the picture are talking. Tell them to write down the dialogue (a maximum of five utterances per person in the picture). Then the students read out their dialogues. It can be fun if the man/boy takes the female role and vice versa when reading the dialogue out.

Variation

Silent dialogues. The following starters (A, B, C, D, E, F) are handed out to different pairs. That means that in a class of twenty-four learners no more than two pairs have the same starter. Each pair proceeds like this: student A copies the starter and student B writes a continuation. Then B hands the piece of paper back to A, who reads what B has written. A then writes a reply and hands the paper back to B, etc. The completed dialogues are read out in class.

Starters:

1. WOMAN: *There's just one little thing you don't know yet. My husband/boyfriend back at the hotel has got his binoculars trained on us.*

2. WOMAN: *What about having dinner together tonight?*
   MAN: *Well, mh, the problem is I've promised my girlfriend to go to the movies with her tonight.*
3. WOMAN: *There's no point in meeting again Jeff.*
4. MAN: *Of course you'll come. No woman has ever said 'No' when I invited her to a party.*
5. MAN: *What about having a cup of tea at my place. I could show you my new computer.*
6. MAN: *I'm sorry, Eileen, but I need someone who understands me, who is willing to listen, who cares for me.*

Sample picture

Action research element

Depending on the age group you teach, it might be necessary to change the starters and go for pictures of teenagers. With some adult groups who were used to creative writing we have found it even more rewarding not to provide any starters for the silent dialogues and to rely completely on the students' imagination stimulated by the pictures.

53 Picture associations

Types of picture:	Any
Skill areas:	Speaking, listening
Vocabulary:	As related to content of pictures
Function:	Discussing personal perception
Level:	Intermediate and above
Time:	20 minutes
Purpose:	To stimulate discussion among the students

Preparation

Cut out lots of pictures at random from newspapers and magazines.

In class

1. Write down the following words on the board and explain their meaning:

   life — love — fun — fear — family — hope — anger — happiness — God — secrets — death — surprise — self — time — other people

2. Display the pictures and ask the students each to choose three of the words on the board, and for each word one picture that they associate with it.

3. Pair up your students and get them to talk about their choices.

> *NOTE: This activity is a combination of an activity we learnt from John Morgan and another by Carlos Maeztu. Sources: S. Lindstroemberg (ed.),* The Recipe Book *(Pilgrims–Longman, 1990), p. 48; C. Sion (ed.),* Recipes for Tired Teachers *(Addison-Wesley, 1985, p. 7).*

54 The most dangerous animal in the world

Types of picture:	Photo of a violent scene taken from a newspaper or magazine
Skill areas:	Reading, speaking, listening, note taking, writing
Functions:	Describing a situation or event
Level:	Intermediate and above
Time:	40 minutes
Purpose:	Interpreting pictures, letter writing

Preparation

Bring along a photo/photos of a scene showing violence. One picture per pair of students. If there is just one picture you should provide each pair with a photocopy.

In class

1. Write the following words in the box on the board and ask your learners to sort them into three lists: (a) people who commit violence: (b) adjectives describing these people, (c) violent actions. Explain that some words might fit into more than one category.

   wound fierce rob mugger strangle furious war battle aggressive fight bully kill hit mug stab murderer murder brutal attack burglar evil criminal knock down thief cruel robber deadly rape shoot gunman beat steal

2. Check the students' results and clarify the meaning of words if necessary.

3. Hand out pictures of scenes showing violence. The learners now try to put each picture into a proper context:

   What has happened before?
   What will happen next?

Who are the people involved?
Where does the scene take place?

Each pair makes notes of their ideas. Then they get together with another pair, show them their picture (this, obviously, need not be done if they are all working on the same picture) and tell the other pair about their ideas. When they have finished, it is the other pair's turn to present their ideas.

Alternative: when different pictures are used: pair A hands their notes and picture to pair B who try to work out pair A's ideas. If there are discrepancies, pair A give their version of the context of the picture. The roles are then reversed.

Variation

The picture(s) are handed out and the students are given the following instructions: imagine that you are on holiday and you happened to take this picture. In a letter, you send the picture to a friend of yours in Britain/the United States explaining to her/him what happened and how you managed to take it.

55 Animals

Types of picture:	Animals
Skill areas:	Listening, speaking
Vocabulary:	Adjectives describing personality
Functions:	Comparing people and animals, talking about other people's character
Level:	Intermediate and above
Time:	50–60 minutes
Purpose:	Students discuss human qualities of character and learn more about how others in a group see themselves

Preparation

Select at least ten pictures of animals and one or two poems on animals. You may want to photocopy these poems for each student in your class.

In class

1. Read out two poems about animals. Alternatively, hand out photocopies of the poems and ask your students to read them and discuss how the poet compares the animal in the poem to a human being.

2. Write down adjectives describing human character on the board, for example:

aggressive	*elegant*	*powerful*	*intelligent*
cynical	*proud*	*strong*	*brave*
friendly	*calm*	*daring*	*considerate*
patient	*shy*	*wise*	*spontaneous*
playful	*soft*	*witty*	*colourful*
lively	*loyal*	*inspiring*	*sensitive*
humorous	*honest*	*devoted*	*energetic*
clever	*greedy*		

3. Learners associate adjectives with animals (in groups of three or four). They note down their associations and then read them out aloud.

4. Arrange your class in a circle. Start with one student. Each member of the group in turn should tell this student what animal they think he/she would be, if he/she were an animal, and why. After explaining the task, give your students enough time to think and make notes about their choices and the reasons for these. If there are more than eight students in your group, form smaller circles.

Example:
Françoise, if you were an animal, I think you would be an owl. You seem to be tired all day and wake up in the evening. And you are also very clever. Whenever you say something, it is something that makes me think.

If necessary, note down language on the board to facilitate your students' conversation, for example:

> *If you were an animal, I think you would be a ... because ...*
> *You seem to be ...*
> *You are ...*
> *Whenever ...*
> *You often ...*

56 Would you call that art?

**Types of
picture:**   Postcards with reproductions of a wide range of paintings

Skill areas: Speaking, listening, writing

Vocabulary: Words related to art

Functions: Making value judgements concerning art; story telling

Level: Advanced

Time: 80 minutes

Purpose: To stimulate discussion, to write dialogues

Preparation

Collect a fairly large number of reproductions of paintings. It does not matter whether you cut them out of art magazines, calendars or collect postcards. There should be a fair number of reproductions of paintings that contain two or more people and also some reproductions of abstract paintings or pictures that may cause considerable discussion due to differences in the learners' attitudes towards them.

In class

1. Ask your class the following questions. Depending on the size of your group, you might want to discuss them in groups or with the whole class.

    Do you like going to galleries? Say why, or why not.
    Are there any pictures on the wall in your bedroom? What are they and what is in them? (paintings, drawings, reproductions, photos, postcards, calendar pictures, posters, cuttings from magazines etc.)
    What pictures are there on the walls in the rest of the house, flat or building you live in? Who chose them? How do you feel about them? Would you change them if you could? If so, what would you have instead?

2. Stick several pictures on the wall which focus on two or more people. Alternatively,

hand out photocopies of the reproductions. Take some white paper and cut out some speech or thought bubbles and arrange them in such a way that the people in the pictures seem to be thinking or speaking like the characters in a cartoon. Ask your learners to work in pairs and to write down (not more than two sentences for each person) what the people in the pictures are saying or thinking. Have them read out the dialogues and decide which they like best.

3.   Choose a picture that lends itself to story telling (the Impressionists and the Expressionists and Symbolists are a good source). Hand out photocopies to each learner. Provide some starters or sentences that should be used as endings, and tell them to write the story behind the picture.

4.   Ask your learners to work in groups of four. Hand out a series of pictures that range from fairly realistic ones to abstract paintings. Tell them to decide for themselves which ones are art and which not. Then get them to consider each picture in turn and discuss whether they think it is art or not.

NOTE: *The ideas have been taken from R. Davis, G. Gerngross, C. Holzmann, H. Puchta and M. Schratz* Make your Way with English *7 (Österreichischer Bundesverlag 1991).*

---

57 Brother tree

Preparation

Cut out pictures of different sorts of tree. Provide the students with copies of the text, 'Respect for trees', by Ghillean T. Prance.

In class

1. Hand out copies of the text below and have your students read it. Get your students to talk briefly about the difference in attitudes towards trees in western societies and that of 'primitive' tribes.

   Respect for trees
   I remember well my first day of botanical field work in the rainforests of Surinam. After a long journey by air, two days by canoe and then two on foot, we reached the area where our expedition was already at work. Near the camp was a huge buttressed flowering tree of Licania *in the plant family* Chrysobalanaceae *on which I had recently completed my doctoral thesis and was especially eager to see and collect dried herbarium specimens. Since the tree was far too large to climb, the expedition leader immediately asked one of our most willing bush negro helpers to cut down this forest giant so that we might collect a few flowering twigs for specimens. The bush negroes are descended from escaped African slaves who rebuilt*

tribal life in the forest of Surinam and are a wonderful people who maintain many of their own traditions. We were all surprised when Frederick refused to fell the tree. After much coaxing, he agreed to cut it down; not immediately but in a few minutes' time and only after he had appeased the 'bushy mama', his deity. After chanting a prayer and making an offering to the bushy mama, Frederick began to cut down the tree, continuing to sing all the time in a loud chant that would show clearly that it was not he who was cutting the tree but the white man, who had ordered him to and who should be blamed for this unnecessary destruction. When these people fell a tree to build a house or to obtain wood for their famous carvings, they will also appease the bushy mama in a similar fashion.

The trees of the forest have a spiritual value to the people and are not their property to destroy. This attitude leads to the protection and more prudent use of resources than in our western society. It is an experience which I have never forgotten and is one of the reasons why I either climb trees or use local tree climbers to collect my plant specimens! It was good to be given this lesson about respect for trees from a native teacher on my very first foray into the rainforest and it has become even more important to me as species of trees in the Amazon become threatened with extinction by deforestation or excessive use.

2. Have your students arrange their seats in a circle. Inform them that you are going to tell them a story and ask them to close their eyes while you do.

Start like this:
Close your eyes and concentrate on your breathing. Breathe in and out very gently and imagine that you are going outside this room. It's a hot day and you are going for a long walk. The land in the part of the country you are in is flat, and only far away can you see something shimmering in the distance. You keep walking and walking (pause) and it's getting hotter and hotter, but finally you see that there is a mountain ahead of you. After a long time (pause) you finally arrive at the foot of the mountain. There is a small brook there from which you drink. You decide to follow the brook and you walk up and up (pause) until you arrive at a flat area. And there in the distance is a single tree. You walk closer and closer, looking at the tree. It's much cooler there and you decide to lie down under the tree. (pause) You look up into the branches and you can feel the cool wind and you feel very, very calm. (pause) And as you listen to the wind (pause) the tree begins to tell its story and it tells you about the times when it was not a tree but a person and how it lived then. (pause) And you listen and dream and dream and listen. (pause) And after a long while (pause) you slowly stand up and you walk down and down the mountain (pause) until you reach the flat part of the country and then you slowly walk back to where you have come from (pause) still thinking of what the tree has told you. (pause) And in a moment I will count to ten. Join me at the count of five, opening your eyes at ten, feeling refreshed and relaxed. One (pause) two (pause) etc.

3. The students share in small, supportive groups what they experienced during the fantasy trip.

4. Stick several pictures of trees on the wall. Ask your students to stand up and carefully look at the trees. Tell them to think of people they have met in their lives until they can match up a person from their lives with one of the pictures of trees. Then the students go back to their seats and make notes.

5. Ask your learners to work in groups. Each member points out the tree they have chosen and then talks about the person that came to their mind.

Variations

1. Your students work in groups. Their task is to tell a story about a tree (felling a tree, climbing a tree, building a tree house, hiding in a tree, etc.). They first make notes and then tell their stories.

2. They write vignettes about trees.

   Example:
   A couple of years ago we travelled through the southwest of the United States. In one of the National Parks we stopped on a mountain pass and went to sit on a rock close to a very old pine tree. Its roots clung to crevices in the rocks, its gnarled branches seemed ready to fight off the rain, the snow and icy wind. I took its picture home with me and whenever I'm faced with a struggle I think of that tough tree at 3,000 metres.

58 Where would you like to live?

Types of picture:	Several photos (preferably in colour) of places where people live (high rise apartment block, cottage, skyscraper, terraced house, farm, in cities, in small towns, in the country, etc.)
Skill areas:	Speaking, listening
Vocabulary:	Buildings
Grammar:	Questions, conditional
Functions:	Asking questions, expressing likes and dislikes
Level:	Lower intermediate and above
Time:	40 minutes
Purpose:	Practising holding interviews

Preparation

Cut out pictures from magazines as specified above.

In class

1. Show your class several pictures of buildings and practise any new words if necessary.

2. Ask your learners to choose the building they would most like to live in and the building they would least like to live in. Tell them to think of three reasons for their choices and to make notes.

3. Get them to work in pairs. A tells his/her partner which buildings s/he has chosen and gives reasons. B takes notes. Then they change roles.

4. Each pair now works with another pair. Each member of the group tells the other pair about his/her partner's choice.

Example:
Barbara would like to live in the skyscraper. She says she would prefer to live in a big city because she loves the exciting life there. She thinks it's much easier to get a good job in a city and there are better schools and hospitals. She would not like to live on a farm because she thinks life in the country is boring. She says she can't stand the smell of farms, and besides, she is allergic to hay.

5. Divide the class into groups of three (A, B, C). A chooses one of the photos. A imagines having lived in this place for a long time. B and C are going to interview A about what it is like to live in the place. Give the class sufficient time to think about what they are going to say and ask. Tell them to make notes.

Then ask them to act out the interviews in front of the class. If, however, the class is very large, get them to do the interviews in small groups and have them then report back to the class.

Sample pictures

59 Picture stories on the overhead projector (OHP)

Types of picture:	Picture stories on transparencies
Skill areas:	Speaking, listening, writing
Functions:	Asking for information, giving information
Level:	Lower intermediate and above
Time:	50 minutes
Purpose:	Eliciting short turn talk

Preparation

Produce transparencies of picture stories and cut out the individual pictures.

In class

There is no such thing as an established order of steps when dealing with picture stories on the OHP. What should be kept in mind is that the emphasis is on eliciting ideas from the learner and not describing pictures. The following steps have worked very well in class. The order in which the steps are listed is arbitrary.

1. Put one picture (transparency) on the OHP, which has not yet been switched on. Get a piece of paper and cut a small hole in it. Place it on the picture and switch the OHP on. Ask your learners to call out what they think they can spot while you slowly move the piece of paper with the hole in its centre over the picture. Finally, remove the piece of paper so that your learners can see the picture.

2. You might also begin a story by showing the second picture and ask them to speculate about the first.

3. Unfocus the OHP. Place a picture on it. Ask your students to guess the content of the blurred picture.

4. Put a picture on the OHP while it is switched off. Tell your learners to concentrate and switch the OHP on for a brief moment only. Elicit ideas from your learners about what they think they have seen. Repeat this step several times before you finally keep the OHP switched on.

5. Put three or four pictures on top of each other. Switch on the OHP and ask them to guess the contents of the pictures.

6. Put all the pictures on the OHP in jumbled order. Ask your learners to tell the story or write it down.

7. Ask your learners to work in pairs (A and B). All the As either close their eyes or turn their chairs round so that they can not see the picture on the OHP. Get the As to ask questions about the picture. These should elicit yes/no answers from the Bs, who are looking at the picture. For the next picture, the As and Bs change roles.

8. The teacher shows one picture, the learners ask questions about the next picture, which they are not yet allowed to see.

9. Tell your class to close their eyes and to visualise the next picture. This is a step that works very well with the end pictures of stories, since they usually contain an element of surprise. Elicit their ideas and then show them the picture.

Sample picture story

Action research element

The picture story above was taught to a class of thirteen-year-old students in their third year of English.

1. The teacher showed picture two and wrote: '*I wish I had/could/was/lived/didn't have to . . .*' on the board. The task for the students was to put themselves into the girl's shoes and to come up with a sentence. The teacher reacted to what the students said.

    Example:
    STUDENT: *I wish I lived in a warmer country.*
    TEACHER: *Are you freezing? Or are you just daydreaming.*
    STUDENT: *It's cold outside and I'm daydreaming of a hot country.*

2. Learners then tried to guess the content of picture 1, guided by the teacher's questions: *Where is the girl? What do you think is happening in picture 1? How does she feel?* Finally, the picture was shown.

3. The class closed their eyes and visualised the next picture. Then the teachers asked them what they had seen on their 'inner TV'.

4. Pictures 3 and 4 were shown and the learners wrote down the dialogue between the magician and the girl. They were told to write not more than three utterances each. The students' texts were then read out in pairs.

5. Picture 5 was shown and again the learners tried to visualise picture 6. The teacher asked for their ideas and then showed picture 6.

6. The class was given a worksheet with the text of the story on it. Below the text there were six sentences. The students' task was to decide which three of the six sentences could be inserted into the text and where.

Sample worksheet

The Magician

Nobody was watching her.
The magician listened carefully.
He looked great in his strange hat and long coat with magic signs on it.
He didn't tell her why it was wrong.
'You have read it', he said.
Half an hour had passed but nobody had come along.

Shirley's car had broken down on a lonely road in Arizona and she was waiting for help. Shirley was daydreaming about a friendly magician, who could say his magic words to make her car all right again. Suddenly she heard someone saying 'Good afternoon'.
And there he was, her magician, standing on a little cloud, raising his hat. Shirley jumped up and told the magician what her problem was. Finally she said, 'I wish I had a beautiful, new car'.
The magician closed his eyes and said some magic words. There were some

flashes of bright light and a lot of smoke, then he sailed up and away on his little cloud. When the smoke had gone, Shirley's old car wasn't there any more. But there was no new car — there was a wonderful carriage on a lonely road in Arizona.

7. For homework the class wrote another ending for the story.

NOTE: *The sample picture story is taken from G. Gerngross, H. Puchta and M. Schratz* What's the story — Fifteen picture stories for the OHP *(Spectra, 1989).*

60 Write a plot

Types of picture:	Photos of people
Skill areas:	Speaking, listening, writing
Vocabulary:	Characteristic features of people
Function:	Describing people
Level:	Intermediate and above
Time:	60 minutes
Purpose:	Practising vocabulary and discussion, creative writing

Preparation

Cut out photos of people from magazines, preferably not film or TV stars.

In class

1. Preteach, if necessary, vocabulary such as: *caring, uncaring, cold, clever, cheerful, considerate, inconsiderate, courageous, timid, energetic, lazy, friendly, unfriendly, generous, miserly, mean, gentle, tough, hard-working, just, unjust, organized, careless, honest, dishonest, cunning, patient, impatient, reliable, unreliable, sensible, unreasonable, nervous, tense, restless, powerful, ambitious, weak, stable, unstable, tactful, tactless, tender, intelligent, stupid,* etc.

2. Hand out four strips of paper (A, B, C, D) to each student. Ask them to write down the following on each strip: A, a made-up name; B, a job; C, an adjective characterising a person's appearance; D, something that is typical of a person's behaviour (see step 1).

    Example: A, Bruce McCallion; B, estate agent; C, tall; D, cunning.

    Collect all the A, B, C, D strips and hand them out again so that everyone gets one A, one B, one C and one D strip.

3. Display the photos of people and ask each of your learners to choose a picture that they think they could match up with what their four strips say.

4. Tell them to write a fully fleshed out description based on their picture and the four strips. They then read it out to the class.

   Example (picture of a woman; the four strips said *Brooke Morales, pilot, slim, ambitious*).
   Her name is Brooke Morales and she is of mixed Canadian and Mexican origin. She has dark hair, a fairly dark complexion, she is very slim and lives in San Diego, California. She has always been interested in aeroplanes and after graduating from high school she got her pilot's licence. She is a very tough and ambitious woman and is now trying to buy herself into a small, but promising private air-service business.

5. Ask your class to take their pictures and personality sketches with them and work in groups of three to four. Then get them to exchange their pictures plus the personality sketches with the group next to them.

6. Each group writes a plot for a film starring the people in the photos and based on the personality sketches. They should have access to more pictures, however, if they need more or different characters for which they would also have to write personality sketches. Each group finally reads out their plot and, at the same time, displays the photos of the 'stars' of their film.

61   Doodles

Types of picture: Blackboard drawings

Skill areas: Listening, speaking

Grammar: Present progressive

Functions: Guessing actions, describing actions

Level: Elementary and above

Time: 20–30 minutes

Purpose: Students practise the present progressive in a game-like way

Preparation

None if drawings are made by the teacher on the board, otherwise drawings done on OHP transparency or on poster paper.

In class

1. Ask your learners if they know what a 'doodle' is. If possible get someone to draw an example on the board. If they have no idea draw the following doodle on the board. While you are drawing try to elicit from your learners what they think this is going to be.

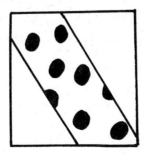

Finally tell them that it is a giraffe passing a window.

2. Present various doodles on the OHP, poster paper or on the board. It might be helpful to note down some chunks of language on the board:

What do you think this drawing shows?
> *I have no idea.*
> *I think it's a/the ... ...ing ...*
> *It could be a/the ... ...ing ...*
> *It could also be a/the ... ...ing ...*

Example:

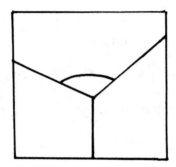

TEACHER: *What do you think this drawing shows?*
STUDENT: *I think it's the moon rising behind two mountains.*
etc.

Solution: It's a bald man reading his paper in the morning, as seen by his wife.

Variation

Students draw their own doodles on A4 paper and ask each other what they think is shown. This could also be done as a competition. For this purpose the students work in groups of four to six. They get a point each for thinking of a new doodle and also for being able to interpret a doodle drawn by another group. It is great fun to get students to come up with lots of different interpretations of one and the same doodle.

Sample drawings

Possible interpretations for the doodles are the following:

A spider doing a handstand.
A cat sitting behind a box.
A candle walking through a tunnel.
A horse standing behind a house.
A mouse standing behind a house.
A snake going upstairs.
A snowman doing a handstand.
A mouse riding a bike.
A worm having a vegetarian meal.
A person in a big hat fishing.

NOTE: *We got the idea for this activity from Detlev and Margarete von Ziegesar,* Kommunikative Grammatikübungen für den Englischunterricht *(Klett, 1981). The doodles above have been taken from our collection of OHP transparencies for practising grammar with secondary learners in G. Gerngross, H. Puchta and M. Schratz,* Grammatische Übungsfolien 1 *(Langenscheidt−Longman, 1988).*

62 Checking listening comprehension

Types of picture:	Picture story
Skill area:	Listening comprehension
Level:	Elementary
Time:	20–30 minutes
Purpose:	Checking listening comprehension

Preparation

Make photocopies of a picture story (or of the sample pictures below). You need one copy of the story for each pair of students. Cut out the individual pictures.

Alternatively prepare a stick-drawing cartoon strip of a story you would like to tell. Make photocopies of these drawings for half the number of your students. Cut up the cartoon strip into single pictures.

In class

1. Preteach any necessary vocabulary.

2. Tell your students the story. Do not read the story out, act it out using mime and gesture to help your learners understand the gist of the story. Talk at a natural pace. Have the students stand in a circle and act the story out too, by imitating your gestures and mime. Tell the story twice in this way.

3. Tell the story a third time and ask your students to close their eyes. Get them to 'watch TV in their heads', that is, to see the story on an imaginary TV screen. You may want to play some soft, meditative music the rhythm of which goes well with the story.

4. Ask your students to work in pairs. Hand out the pictures to them and get them to put the pictures in front of them on their desks. Do not give them any time to order the pictures, but tell the story a fourth time. Their task is to hold up any picture that they think corresponds with the stage of the story as told by you.

While you are telling the story check if your learners are holding up the correct pictures. If a learner has got the wrong picture, do not go on with the story, but repeat what you have just said. Go on only after the learner has put up the correct picture.

5. Ask your learners to 'reconstruct' the story by putting the pictures into the correct order.

Sample story

Jack works for a farmer — farmer gives him some money — on his way home Jack drops it into river — mother angry, says, 'Put it into your pocket!'

Works for baker — gives him a cat — puts it into pocket — on his way home cat jumps out, runs away — mother angry, says, 'Pull it along'.

Works for butcher — gives him sausage — pulls it along — dog comes — eats it up — mother angry — Silly Jack — No money, no cat, no sausage!

Action research element

We have used this activity, in combination with the suggestion on how to introduce vocabulary to beginners on page 15, in primary school classes.

Words and phrases pretaught with the help of simple board drawings were: *cat/dog/river/butcher/sausage/baker/farmer/silly/angry/money/put in pocket/drop/pull along.*

NOTE: *The story is an adaptation of the folk tale 'Lazy Jack'. The version given in the sample pictures had been taken from the textbook* Conrad and Company *for teaching English as a foreign language in primary schools. Source: E. Ballinger, G. Gerngross, R. Hladnig, H. Puchta,* Conrad and Company *vol. 2 (Österreichischer Bundesverlag, 1991).*

Index of activities by picture type

Index of skills

Index of proficiency level